IKEBANA

IKEBANA

THE ART OF JAPANESE FLOWER ARRANGING

■ELIZABETH PALMER■

CHARTWELL
BOOKS, INC.

■ BIBLIOGRAPHY

The Floral Art of Japan
Josiah Condor
1891
(Read to the Asiatic Society of Japan, 13 March 1889 under the title 'Theory of Japanese Flower Arrangements')

Zen in the Art of Flower Arrangement
Gustie L Herrigel, tr R F C Hall
1958

Flower Arrangement the Ikebana Way
Ed Dr William Steer Shufunotomo
1962
(Includes 'The History of Ikebana by Monobu Ohi, tr Seiko Aoyama)

The Master's Book of Ikebana
Ed Donald Richie & Meredith Weatherby
1966

Ikebana Spirit and Technique
(from Ikebana-Praxis – 1976, J Neumann-Neudamm)
Shusui Komoda & Horst Pointer
Blandford 1980

A QUINTET BOOK

Published by Chartwell Books
A Division of Booksales, Inc.
110 Enterprise Avenue
Secaucus, New Jersey 07094

Copyright © 1988 Quintet Publishing Limited.
All rights reserved. No part of this publication may be reproduced, stored in a retrieval system or transmitted in any form or by any means, electronic, mechanical, photocopying, recording or otherwise, without the permission of the copyright holder.

ISBN 1-55521-415-0

This book was designed and produced by
Quintet Publishing Limited
6 Blundell Street
London N7 9BH

Designer: Peter Bridgewater
Editors: Caroline Beattie, Patricia Bayer
Horticultural Editor: Sue Phillips
Photography: Will White
Illustrations: Claire Russell

Typeset in Great Britain by Central Southern Typesetters, Eastbourne
Manufactured in Hong Kong by Regent Publishing Services Limited
Printed in Hong Kong by Leefung-Asco Printers Limited

■ CREDITS

In the making of this book I would like to thank my mother, who instilled into me her love of flowers and growing plants; the friends and colleagues whose arrangements grace the pages of this book and who shared with me their store of ikebana knowledge; John and Hilde Woodman, from whose garden material for many of the arrangements was gathered; my teachers and students who journey with me on the way of flowers; and Caroline Beattie, who has not only been a sympathetic and supportive editor but who has also become a friend.

Arrangements made by:

Tricia Hill, Associate Master Ichiyo school: pages 56, 61(bottom), 63(bottom), 65(top), 66(right), 78–79, 97, 111, 122(left).

Angie Jameson, Sogetsu school, Ikebana Centre London: pages 58, 61(top), 62, 64, 66(left), 76–77.

Elizabeth Palmer, Sogetsu school, Ikebana Centre London: back cover, pages 5, 21, 22, 47–55, 57, 59, 60, 63(top), 65(bottom), 67–69, 74–75, 97, 98, 99, 123(left).

Kiyoko Sawada-Rudd, Master Ikenobo school: pages 81–83.

Takashi Sawano, Master Sogetsu school: pages 100–110.

Sumie Takahashi, Masker Koryu school: pages 84–85, 86–96.

Hilde Woodman, Master Ohara school: front cover, pages 112–121, 122(right), 123(right).

Technical pictures: Elizabeth Palmer

Hands used in photographs: Kiyoko Sawada-Rudd and Sumie Takahashi

The picture on page 9 was lent by Sotheby's, London and the picture on page 19 was lent by the Japan Information Centre, London.

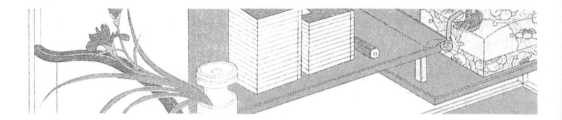

■ CONTENTS

■ INTRODUCTION

Above A humourous drawing of a lesson at the Ikenobo school of Ikebana in the late nineteenth century.

This book aims to provide a practical and pleasurable introduction to the art of Japanese flower arrangement. It describes the techniques involved and the equipment needed, suggests suitable flowers and branches, and gives tips on treatment to extend their vase life.

It also discusses the origins and development of *ikebana*, the philosophy and aesthetic principles underlying the art, and its current practice. The arrangements in the book fall into three categories. First, the basic arrangements are explained and illustrated step-by-step. Following these are variations and ideas for quick and easy arrangements using widely available material.

Secondly, there are examples of classical arrangements to set the historical background and place the work in context. Since these arrangements require a high degree of skill and the guidance of a teacher, no attempt is made to give instruction. This section includes traditional seasonal and festival arrangements.

Then there are free-style arrangements, some requiring little skill and relying on striking material or imaginative containers for their impact; others being more demanding. They range from small arrangements to works of considerable size and are included in the hope that they will stimulate and inspire you to experiment in a spirit of creative play to create your own free-style arrangements.

■ WHAT IS IKEBANA?

The word comes from *ikiru* (to live) and *hana* (flowers and branches); thus it means 'living flowers'. Ikebana is the Japanese art of arranging flowers according to rules and principles evolved over its long history. Ikebana is also a *dō*, a path or way of self-realization. To take up ikebana is to embark on a journey of self-exploration.

Ikebana springs from a response to the beauty and infinite variety of natural plant forms, a recognition of the strength, delicacy and ephemerality of the living flowers and branches that it uses. It can be a hobby or pastime, but for many ikebana becomes an absorbing study leading to a deeper and deeper insight into an understanding of life, its contradictions and their resolution in recognition and acceptance.

Ikebana is as varied as the people who practise it. Traditionally only natural material was used, but contemporary ikebana, responding to change, often incorporates dry material, metal, paper, cloth, glass or plastic. Some modern arrangements even use no fresh material at all.

Sometimes derogatively referred to as 'two sticks and a flower' by those who understand little about it, ikebana can be grand and elaborate, as in the great *rikka* arrangements that evolved in the 16th

Left Upper-class women arranging flowers (late eighteenth century). Note the attention to detail in the picture.

century. The 20th century has, under the leadership of modern masters like Sofu Teshigahara and Houn Ohara, witnessed the development of massive *taisaku* constructed from huge tree trunks, metal, stone and plastic, the results being more akin to sculpture than to the conventional idea of a flower arrangement.

Some designs, like the classical *seika isshu-ike* arrangements made from a single material, are monochromatic and austere, others colourful and exuberant and yet others, like *chabana* (flowers arranged for the tea ceremony), simple and modest. Chabana is perhaps the style most immediately accessible to most Westerners.

Anyone can learn to do ikebana: it must be approached receptively without *trying* too hard. Ikebana requires an intuitive response to the material as well as a grasp of the rules for placing the branches and flowers and, of course, the physical skills to do this securely and correctly. It is one of many techniques developed over the centuries by the Japanese for restoring their sense of *wa* or inner harmony. You begin by looking at the flowers and branches, noticing their shape, the way they grow, how they absorb or reflect light; feeling the strength and suppleness of the branches in your hands; breathing in their scent; recognizing and responding to their uniqueness so that you will be able to show this in your arrangement. You let them 'speak' to you, let the right side of the brain come into play so that you are in touch with your own — perhaps unacknowledged — creativity. In this regard, ikebana is both a therapy and a form of meditation.

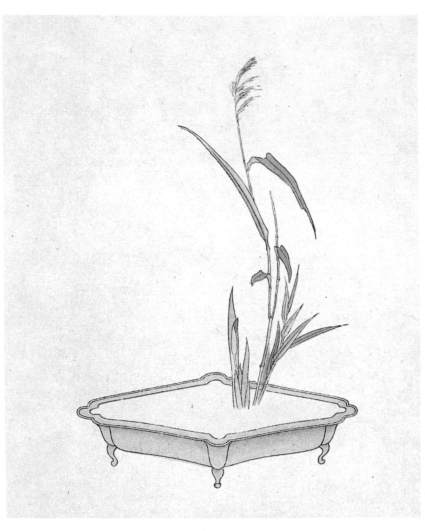

| **Above** A flower seller. The flowers in her basket are easily recognizable as flowers sold today. | **Above right** A Shoka Shofutai arrangement, by Senjo Ikenobo. |

■ THE WAY OF FLOWERS

The original name for ikebana was *ka-dō*, the Way of Flowers. In Japan the pursuit of any art or skill, whether it be archery, martial arts or flower arrangement, is seen as a path leading to potential self-realization. Hence the names *kyu-dō*, the way of archery; *aiki-dō, ju-dō* and *karate-dō*, the ways of martial arts; *cha-dō*, the way of tea; *ken-dō*, the way of the sword, and so on.

In taking up any of these you have to study and master:

■ the physical and technical skills required, which are called *jutsu*. (In ikebana these are the techniques for cutting, shaping and fixing the material in the correct position.)

■ the theory and history, known as *gaku*, and

■ the philosophy involved in the metaphysical and spiritual journey to discover who we really are. This is dō.

The first two can be studied and mastered in a limited time. Dō, how-ever, is a life study.

ORIGINS OF IKEBANA

The roots of ikebana lie in the deep feeling the Japanese have for landscape, their awe of the power of nature manifested in mountains, rocks, waterfalls and trees, and their response to the strength, fragility and beauty of the trees and flowers of their native islands. These feelings expressed themselves in the indigenous religion, *Shintō*, a form of nature-worship.

THE FIRST ARRANGEMENTS

Trees that remain green throughout the bitter winter months seemed to the early Japanese imbued with some mysterious power. Evergreen branches were brought to Shintō shrines as offerings to the *kami*, or nature spirits, worshipped there. It fell to the priests attending these shrines to prolong the life of these offerings by arranging them in vases on the altar.

BUDDHISM

Buddhism reached the shores of Japan via China and Korea in the 6th century and was adopted as the official religion in AD 594. This did not, however, involve the extinction of the indigenous religion; rather, however, Buddhism coexisted with and was influenced by Shintoism. With Buddhism came the custom of offering flowers in vases in front of the image of the Buddha. Thus, the first arrangers were priests. Today you can still see arrangements of flowers and branches, either large and elaborate or simple and unsophisticated, in Shintō shrines and Buddhist temples.

FLOWERS IN EVERYDAY LIFE

Flowers also played an important part in secular life. In the *Minakuchi* (Water Gate) Festival, during the rice-planting season, bunches of flowers were laid at the gates that let the water in to flood the paddy fields; these were to ensure a good harvest. At Tanabata (the summer Star Festival) flowers would be floated down the rivers, while at New Year *kadomatsu* (decorations of pine, bamboo, paper and rope made from rice straw) were placed at the entrance to welcome the spirit of the incoming year. These customs are still practised today.

THE IKENOBO SCHOOL

However, it was in the temples – and in the Rokkakudo Temple in Kyoto in particular – that formal rules for flower arranging evolved. Early in the 7th century, Ono-no-Imoko, a diplomat in China, retired and became head priest of the Rokkakudo Temple. Taking the name

Above This print by Harunobu (d. 1770) shows two women on a lotus pond, one of them picking blossoms.

Senmu, he built a small hut beside a pond *(ike-no-bō)* in the temple grounds. Here his duties included arranging the flower offerings. Senmu is regarded as the first headmaster of the Ikenobō School of ikebana, which takes its name from his simple dwelling.

■ FIRST RECORDS

The earliest records of flower arranging are paintings, stone engravings and artefacts such as bronze vases decorated with lotus flowers. Flower festivals were common in the late 14th century, and flower competitions became popular among the aristocracy in the 15th century. The earliest extant text to deal specifically with ikebana dates from the late 15th century. From then on an increasing number of books were written on the subject.

■ TATEBANA

Flowers were one of the three traditional offerings *(mitsugusoku)* to Buddha, together with candles and incense. In these offerings the material was arranged standing in a narrow-mouthed vase. The erect position expressed the hope that the donor's prayer, like the flowers, would rise toward heaven. In contemporary drawings of this *tatebana* (standing-flower) style, there are three characteristics still found in ikebana today:

a the material emerges from a single point in the container
b the flowers and branches reach upward
c there are three lines with a common focal point that form a triangle

■ RIKKA

Indigenous Japanese arts flourished in the Azuchi-Momoyama Period (1573-1600). The nobility were building more spacious houses and to suit their larger rooms the tatebana style grew in size and complexity, reflecting the current taste for gorgeous display and evolving into a new style called *rikka*. Rikka is an elaborate, formal style using a wide variety of material and representing a symbolic landscape. Strict rules govern the proportions and movement of the branches and the type of material used for each part. Rikka arrangements, made in formal bronze containers, range in size from a modest 2ft/60cm to towering feats of engineering up to 10ft/3m in height. A fascinating subject, rikka requires a volume unto itself.

Although ikebana continued to be the concern of the priestly class, its practice was spreading at the court and among the nobility and the *samurai*. Around this time the new profession arose, *dobōshu*, arbiters of taste who selected and supplied works of art, arranged flowers and designed gardens. Among these was Soami, creator of the famous Zen garden at Ryōanji in Kyoto.

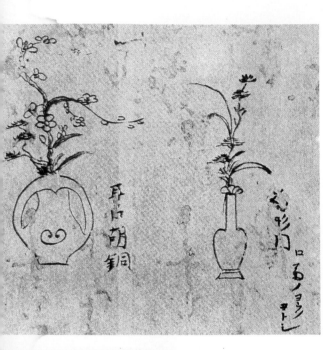

Above These drawings from a text illustrating tatebana (standing flowers style) show how the material should reach up towards heaven. This movement remains typical of ikebana, particularly of the main line in an arrangement.

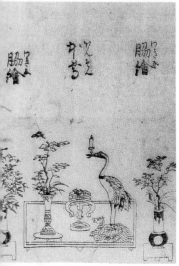

Left Early print showing mitsugusoku, the traditional three-fold offering of flowers, incense and candles (fire) which was made to Buddha. The flowers are arranged tatebana style with the vase on a small kadai. Two further arrangements stand on either side.

風薫 百合花
雨冷 鐵蕉葉
枡抛 瓶裏看
坐臥 幽情憶

大小風玉芝社中

岡本芝仙

| **Left** These two nageire arrangements in a double-mouthed bamboo vase have an engaging simplicity. Note that flowers are placed in the lower position with branches in the upper mouth as they would be in a single arrangement, and how the artist has caught the feeling of the flowers leaning forward. | **Above** A late 18th century print showing visitors studying rikka arrangements made for Tanabata (the Star Festival, 7 July). Notice the tatami matting covering the floor.

■ NAGEIRE-BANA

Parallel to the development of rikka, and partly in reaction to its for-mality and complexity, a natural style known as *nageire-bana* (thrown-in flowers), using simple cylindrical bamboo or ceramic containers, was practised. Nageire is an informal style using only two or three kinds of material and emphasizing the natural form of the flowers and branches. These smaller, simpler arrangements suited a more domestic architec-ture that arose, influenced by the great reforming tea master, Sen-no-Pikyu (1521-1591)

■ THE TEA CEREMONY

Tea drinking was introduced from China in the 8th century. From the 12th century *matcha*, the powdered green tea used in the tea cere-mony, was drunk by Zen monks to help them stay alert during *Zazen* (sitting meditation).

Tea drinking was popular among the nobility, who used it as an opportunity to display and enjoy beautiful and expensive works of art. Reacting against the ostentation and superficiality of this attitude, Sen-no-Rikyu built a simple 3½-mat room where he could serve tea to two or three guests. The entrance to the room was so low that guests had to kneel to enter. It was too narrow to admit an armed man, so swords had to be unbuckled and left outside. By means of this simple device the tea room became, in an age of violence and rigid class distinction, the one place where all could meet without fear and where rank counted little. Here Rikyu worked out the form of tea ceremony still widely followed today.

The tea ceremony as reformed by Rikyu is a unique ritual for restoring a sense of calm and inner harmony. Guests sit quietly in a small room where all colour is subdued and even the light softened, filtered through the *shoji* (paper screens) on the window. Attention focuses entirely on what is happening within this space, on the beautiful quiet movements of the host preparing and serving the tea. In this still atmosphere the senses become alert, responding to the murmur of water heating in an iron kettle on the central hearth, the steam that rises and dissolves in the motionless air, the sunlight and shadow patterning the paper screen, the modest flower breathing in its simple vase beside the scroll hanging in the *tokonoma*. The pressures of life, its stresses and strains are momentarily forgotten.

■ CHABANA

The style known as chabana (tea flowers) developed to fit this mood and setting. It uses simple containers of natural materials; bamboo, gourds, baskets, and rustic ceramics either unglazed or matt-glazed in subdued colours. Flowers are seasonal, unscented, inconspicuous.

In the 16th and 17th centuries, the appreciation and practice of chabana and nageire spread through society with the practice of the tea ceremony.

■ SEIKA (SHOKA)

Toward the end of the 18th century, a new style evolved combining some of the simplicity of nageire with formal aspects taken from rikka. This was the *seika* or *shoka* style. Like rikka, seika has *shin* (formal), *gyo* (semiformal) and *so* (informal) moods, but uses a more restricted range of materials than rikka. Strict rules govern the proportions, placement and direction of the material; this aspect derives from rikka, while the limitation of material comes from nageire. Sometimes two, three or as many as five different types of flowers and branches may be used in one arrangement, but often an arrangement is made entirely from one type of material, such as broom, aspidistra leaves or narcissus. These *isshu-ike*, or arrangements made from only one kind of material, have an austerity that shows the influence of Zen.

Above This seika arrangement in a Chinese-style bronze container has some of the formality of rikka in the carefully controlled placing and shaping of the material. The heaven, man and earth lines are clearly seen. However the use of only two kinds of material shows the influence of nageire.

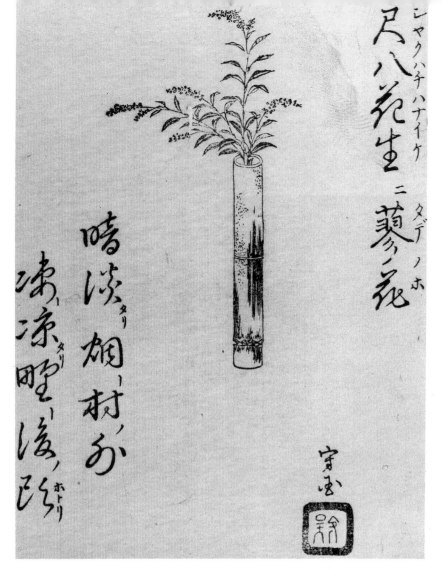

Above, left A chabana in a small bamboo vase to hang on the pillar at the side of the tokonoma during a tea ceremony.

Above Two instructional rikka diagrams; on the left showing how the material is placed and on the right showing the landscape the material symbolizes, such as mountains, trees, a valley, a river, etc.

■ ZEN

Zen Buddhism was introduced to Japan from China by the monk Eisai in AD1191. In Japan it developed into an austere and uniquely Japanese form of Buddhism. Zen holds that forms and rituals are meaningless and words little help in reaching the Buddhist aim of enlightenment. Instead, it uses many techniques to achieve this end, to 'shock' and shake us out of the expectations and patterns of thought that imprison us. The best-known of these is the *koan*, or baffling question, such as "What is the sound of one hand clapping?" – which, of course, has no rational answer. The breakthrough, if it comes, is a flash of enlightenment breaking the trap of logical thought. The sand and stone Zen gardens are similar aids. Faced with their subtle simplicity and the enigma of their silent statement, the mind may loosen its grip and allow light to flood in.

One of the great war lords of the time, hearing that the fence in Sen-no-Rikyu's garden was ablaze with morning glories, sent word that he would come and see the sight. He arrived to find the fence stripped of every flower. Furious, he entered the tea house, prepared to give vent to his wrath. But the words died in his throat, for there in the tokonoma was one perfect blossom. In that instant, confronted with its fragile beauty, he understood. Ikebana, too, can teach the wordless lessons of Zen.

Right This page of *manga* sketches by Hokusai (1760–1849) shows, amongst other things, a monk arranging iris in a bronze bowl. Stones are used to hold the flowers in place and he is arranging the flowers from behind.

■ IKEBANA SCHOOLS

Over the centuries, many ikebana schools grew up in Kyoto. From the middle of the 18th century, they were established in the economically dynamic cities of Osaka and Edo (Tokyo) as well. While many of these schools were associated with temples, increasingly new ones were founded by gifted and enterprising arrangers who wanted to branch out on their own and develop new ideas. Among the best known of these are the *Enshū* School, the *Koryu* School, the *Misho* School and the *Kōdo* School. These were run by an *iemoto* or headmaster, who trained teachers and assistants to work under him. They graded students according to their ability and issued certificates.

In this way, ikebana grew from being the preserve of priests to becoming an aristocratic pastime, a recreation for battle-weary samurai and then a leisure interest of the merchant class. It was only in the 19th century, however, that the term ikebana came into use to refer to the art.

■ THE OPENING OF JAPAN TO THE WEST

When the United States sent in ships in 1867, forcing Japan to open its doors to the West, the effect upon the country was immediate and dramatic. New ideas, new products, books and knowledge began to flow into the country. People travelled abroad and encountered different ways of life. The government adopted a deliberate policy of encouraging women to enter fields that had previously been male preserves, among them ikebana. For while women had practised ikebana in their homes and, indeed, ikebana was considered a necessary accomplishment for *geisha*. Masters had always been men and women were not taken seriously either as arrangers or teachers.

Two other important factors affecting ikebana at the time were the influence of Western architecture on domestic interiors and the introduction of new plants and flowers to Japan. People who redecorated a room in their house in the Western style found that they needed arrangements to fit into this setting. Arrangements designed for the tokonoma, which were only seen from the front by people seated on the floor, were obviously unsuitable for being put on a table and viewed from more than one side by people sitting on chairs.

The first to respond to this challenge was Ushin Ohara, who founded the Ohara school in 1895. He created the new *moribana* (piled up flowers) style, made in a shallow, flat-bottomed container, and pioneered the use of more colourful Western flowers in ikebana. Later other schools were established, notably the Sogetsu School, founded by Sofu Teshigahara (whose interest in sculpture deeply influenced his ikebana); the Adachi School, founded by Choka Adachi, the first to run correspondence courses in ikebana, and the Ichiyo, which specialized in courses for foreigners both in Japan and abroad, where tuition was by correspondence backed up by short courses.

Above A seika arrangement of three peonies stands on a box behind these two geisha preparing to receive visitors in this *ukiyoe* print by Shigemasa Kitao (1740–1809).

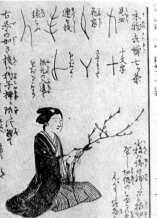

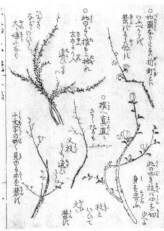

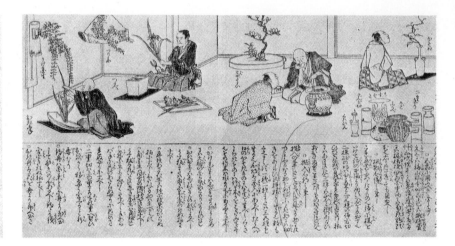

Above Sketches and notes on trimming and shaping branches.

Above, right Preparing for an exhibition. On the left two men are working on seika arrangements with their completed hanging arrangements already in place nearby. Behind the two figures engaged in conversation is an arrangement in a large shallow dish. A fifth figure contemplates a finished piece. Note the selection of containers on right.

■ THE SPREAD OF IKEBANA

During the Occupation of Japan after World War II, Americans and British people lived in Japan in large numbers for the first time. Wives who accompanied their husbands had leisure time to explore the arts and culture of Japan. Many took up ikebana, some of them seriously to qualify as teachers. These women spread the knowledge of ikebana when they returned home.

In 1956, Mrs Ellen Gordon Allen, the wife of an American general, founded Ikebana International in Tokyo. Its motto, 'Friendship through flowers', expresses its aim of fostering international amity through the study of ikebana. I.I., as it is familiarly known, now has chapters and study groups throughout the world, which hold meetings and workshops, give demonstrations and organize exhibitions.

The Tokyo headquarters (GPO Box 1262, Tokyo, Japan) publishes an excellent quarterly magazine and arranges demonstration tours by headmasters. Regional and international conferences are held in different centres, with a convention in Japan ever five years. Your local Japanese Embassy or Consulate should be able to tell you about your nearest I.I. chapter and of ikebana teachers in your area.

With the economic growth of Japan, more and more people have had the opportunity of living, working or studying in Japan, or have come to know Japanese living abroad. The ease of international travel also makes it possible for many more to visit the country whose economic and cultural influence on the rest of the world shows little sign of abating. Our roads are filled with Japanese cars and there can be few homes without a Japanese radio, television, sound system, washing machine or other appliance. Japanese influence on fashion, design and architecture is immeasurable and ikebana is particularly suited to the simple, clean lines and uncluttered feel of contemporary style. Ikebana also recognizes the importance of our need to learn to live in harmony with nature — which connects it to some of the most pressing issues of our time.

Left Behind the woman in this early painting you can see a tokonoma with a simple arrangement of flowers and grasses on a plain kadai in front of a painted scroll.

■ CHARACTERISTICS OF IKEBANA

Right Ink painting of bamboo showing the application of the principle of asymmetry and the incorporation of space into the design.

Ikebana is an art and discipline with a long history and considerable body of literature. The aesthetic principles that govern it are characteristic of Japanese art in general, so it would be enlightening to consider some of the differences between Japanese and Western art, by looking at specific examples of the two.

In architecture, for instance, a good comparison can be made between the pyramids or the Parthenon and a Japanese building like the Byodo-in or Phoenix Hall at Uji near Kyoto. It is immediately apparent that the Western structures dominate the landscape and are visible from a great distance. In addition they are built of stone and intended to last, to conquer time as well as space.

On the other hand, the Phoenix Hall lies hidden behind walls, and so well does it blend in with surrounding nature, that once within these walls it is only discovered when one approaches near enough to see it among the trees that overtop it. Wooden pillars support graceful, clay-tiled roofs so that it seems to float above its image reflected in the lake in front. The lake is really only a large pond but the proportions of lake and building, and the relationship between them, are so perfect that both seem much larger.

Built around AD 1050, Phoenix Hall is considerably younger than the Parthenon, 447-438 BC, and many of the buildings that once surrounded it have been destroyed by fire. While geography and natural resources must have influenced the choice of site and building materials in both cases, the Japanese building nevertheless sees man as existing in harmony with nature rather than trying to dominate it. All the measurements are on a human scale and recognize the inevitability of change and decay. In fact, the great wooden buildings of Japan are recreated at intervals by craftsmen using the same materials and skills and following exactly the pattern of the originals.

Ikebana, in choosing to work with essentially ephemeral materials, accepts the transience of all things and in attempting to express their essence, acknowledges man's place in nature. This attitude is explicitly stated in the names given to the three main lines in an arrangement: *ten, chi, jin,* that is, heaven, earth, man.

Western flower arrangement relies very much on massed flowers for its impact, presenting a completed work to be admired. It places the most gorgeous, fully opened flower at the centre, making it the focal point. Ikebana uses line and space and by making the viewer the focal point, draws us in and invites us to share in the creative act.

Above The Phoenix Hall or Byodo-in at Uji, near Kyoto. Built around 1050 it harmonises perfectly with the surrounding trees and seems to float above its reflected image.

Briefly the main characteristics of ikebana are the following:

▌ **Not just Decoration** Ikebana is an art and a discipline leading to self-awareness.

▌ **Asymmetric Balance** Ikebana uses asymmetric balance, a balance of 30/70 as opposed to the 50/50 balance of mainstream Western art.

▌ **In and Yō** It also uses the principle of *in* and *yō* (yin and yang), which recognizes opposites as balancing and completing each other; thus, day balances and completes night; male, female; space, mass and so on.

▌ **Ephemerality** Ikebana acknowledges and embodies ephemerality, the transience of all things. An arrangement should always include a bud, holding promise of the future, and perhaps a damaged or fading leaf to remind us of the past.

▌ **Space** Space forms an integral part of the arrangement. This space is not mere emptiness but a dynamic element in the composition.

▌ **Upward Movement** The material is arranged to follow the line of growth, moving upward toward the sun.

▌ **Three-Dimensionality** Arrangements are three-dimensional. The material reaches forward toward the viewer, who is the focal point of the arrangement.

▌ **Understatement** By taking away, for instance, trimming side branches and leaves to reveal line, or selecting only a few flowers – along the lines of the 'less is more' principle – rather than adding more material, a stronger and more powerful effect is achieved.

■ FINDING A SETTING

The question of where to place an arrangement needs to be considered carefully. Since ikebana was designed for a traditional Japanese setting, we should understand what that is like.

■ TRADITIONAL SETTING

A traditional Japanese house uses natural materials. The supporting framework and often the ceiling are made from wood. The main walls may be painted a soft neutral colour or, in the case of older and simpler houses, may sometimes be left the colour of the earth used in their structure. The wood may be polished to bring up the grain and the walls smoothed with plaster, but otherwise these are left undecorated so that the subtle colours and textures of the materials can be appreciated.

On one or more sides of the house runs a wide wooden veranda with overhanging eaves. The screens that give access to this can slide back and open the house to the garden, framing it like a picture. In warm weather the veranda becomes an extension of the room.

Light filters through the translucent *shoji* paper that covers these screens and the windows, while thicker opaque paper is used on the *fusuma*, the sliding screens that divide and allow versatility in the use of the interior space.

On the floor are *tatami* mats of firmly packed rice straw, 1¾-2½ in/ 4.4-6.3 cm thick, covered with finely woven grass and edged with a dark border of tape. These mats are a standard size, usually 3 by 6 ft/ 90 by 180 cm, and are laid on the floor in a geometric pattern, making a clean, warm and decorative surface. Rooms are measured in mats and are thus described as a 3-mat room, a 4½-mat room, an 8-mat room and so on.

Furniture is kept to a minimum – a low table, perhaps a *tansu* (chest of drawers) and a screen. People sit on cushions and at night sleep on a *futon* on the floor. When not in use these are packed away and stored out of sight in cupboards behind sliding doors. The result is a harmonious, quietly elegant and largely empty space.

■ THE TOKONOMA

The walls of the room are bare, the only place where a painting or ornament may be placed being the *tokonoma*. This is a recessed space to one side of the room, usually 3 ft/90 cm deep, 6 ft/180 cm high and 3 or 6 ft/90 or 180 cm wide, and having a slightly raised floor. Supporting one side of the tokonoma is a wooden or bamboo post left in its natural shape.

Above An eighteenth-century woodblock print from the Gosetsu hana-awase (five-flower subjects) series by Kitagawa Utamaro. A geisha, whose hasami are similar to those still used today, is using iris from the tray beside her to make a seika arrangement. Note the iris design on the sleeves of her kimono.

This alcove is the focal point of the room. Here a scroll with a painting appropriate to the season, or a poem or wise saying to suit the occasion and written in bold or delicate strokes, will be hung. Below it or to one side a single cherished object may be displayed. These things are brought out from the storage cupboard to be enjoyed with fresh eyes for a short spell.

This is also where the flower arrangement is placed, either on the floor with the material leaning forward toward the viewer, or hanging on the post at the side. The whole of the tokonoma is seen as an exercise in balancing the scroll, the ikebana and any object displayed so that they form a pleasing design. The material for the arrangement is chosen and arranged to complement its companions.

■ IKEBANA IN A WESTERN SETTING

There is usually much more to distract the eye in a Western home. Therefore, if the result is to be a happy one, it is necessary when making the arrangement to give the same thought and attention to the relationship with its setting.

Before you begin to work, decide where it is to go. Try to find a plain background or one that will not interfere too much with the lines of the arrangement. Make enough room around the arrangement in order for it to exist in its own space.

Each style has a right- and left-hand form. Choose the appropriate one, as explained in the instructions. If an arrangement is placed in a high position, or a low one, the lines may need to be adjusted. Choose your colours to suit the tones in the room.

It is a good idea to make the arrangement *in situ*, since you can then consider its relationship to its surroundings while working. It also saves having to move it, which can be a tricky, heart-in-mouth operation.

Above Basic Slanting moribana arrangement with flowers and branches made to go in a low position.

Above, left The same Basic Slanting arrangement with material adjusted for placement at a higher level.

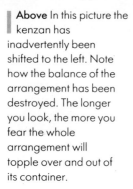

Above In this picture the kenzan has inadvertently been shifted to the left. Note how the balance of the arrangement has been destroyed. The longer you look, the more you fear the whole arrangement will topple over and out of its container.

Above right Showing the relationship between the arrangement and a nearby painting. Note how the yellow solidaster used as filler material picks up the yellow in the watercolour.

■ A FEW SUGGESTIONS

Flowers in the hall greet visitors and welcome people returning home. A table, cabinet or shelf here is a good place for ikebana. For a party you could extend your welcome with branches and flowers in a pot or jug in your porch or on the landing outside your front door. Where space is limited you might find a location where you can hang an arrangement.

The most common place for flowers is in the room where we entertain or relax. But many living rooms get rather crowded. Apart from the furniture and the pictures on the walls, there is the bric-a-brac we all tend to accumulate. Perhaps you will need to clear a space before your flowers can 'repose peacefully' and thus be seen to full advantage.

Flowers on the table during a meal are always appreciated. You will find examples of arrangements for the dinner table elsewhere in this book, including some ideas for quick and easy-to-make ones.

A small arrangement in the guest room is a welcoming touch, but why not have some in the places where you spend lots of time – in the kitchen, on your desk or worktable, or in your bedroom? If surface space is at a premium, and it usually is, then try putting a few flowers in a wall-hung vase or small basket.

A landing is also a good place for an arrangement. In summer you could float a few flowers in a bowl on the floor; in cooler weather, stand a taller vase in a corner.

In Japan there is often a miniature arrangement in the toilet or bathroom. This is a nice touch in what is often one of the few places we can be alone to think our own thoughts. The surprise of finding flowers in unexpected places adds considerably to the pleasure they give.

■ EQUIPMENT

All tasks are easier and more pleasurable with the right equipment. The tools and other items described here are especially designed for ikebana. Anyone with a serious interest in studying ikebana should consider acquiring at least a *kenzan* and *hasami*. They will prove a good investment.

Very little outlay is needed to start practising ikebana. For your first arrangement, which will be a moribana style, you will need a shallow, flat-bottomed container, preferably a dark colour, 8–12in/20–30cm in diameter and about 2in/5cm deep. A suitable dish can be found in most households. Then you will need something to cut with. Initially, you could get by with a combination of florist's or other scissors to cut the flowers and a pair of secateurs for the branches.

The third thing you will need is a kenzan, or pinholder. This is something you are less likely to have and, since it cannot be improvised it will probably be your first purchase.

■ KENZANS OR PINHOLDERS

A *kenzan* (from *ken*, meaning sword, and *zan*, mountain) consists of a heavy leaden base with strong, sharp steel needles to support the flowers and branches embedded in it. Pinholders for Western flower arrangements are not designed to be used with branches and are generally neither strong nor heavy enough for ikebana. A Japanese kenzan will prove the better investment.

Kenzans come in a variety of shapes and sizes, from tiny round *gokumame* (barely ½in/1.5cm in diameter), for miniature arrangements or holding a single flower in a floating arrangement, to weighty *gokudaimaru*, measuring 5in/12.7cm across and capable of supporting heavy branches. The most convenient shapes are round and rectangular. A quarter-circle fits snugly into the corner of a rectangular container or against the curve of a round one. Linked kenzans, like the poetically named *nichi-getsu* (sun and moon, a circle and crescent) kenzan, give three kenzans in one. Joined they make one large kenzan, separated you have two smaller ones. This makes them a good buy.

Your first kenzan should be at least 3in/7.6cm in diameter, otherwise it will not be heavy enough to support the material. The shape you choose should suit the container you plan to use with it. A point to consider when selecting a kenzan is the spacing of the needles. At first, avoid one where these spaces are either very closely or very widely spaced. The former are useful when using thin stems, like freesias and spray carnations, or soft stems, like tulips and iris; the

Above *Selection of Kenzans and Shippo* From top left: shippo/kenzan; kenzan with cross of wider spaced needles; tiny round gokumame for miniature arrangements; linked sun and moon kenzan; linked rectangles with differently spaced needles; large round gokudaimaru; long, thin rectangle; quarter-circle; 3in/7.6cm rectangle; sun and moon separated.

latter are easier for fixing thick branches. You will be using a mixture of material. Some kenzans have a central cross of widely spaced needles with more closely spaced needles in between. This is a practical solution.

■ SHIPPO

Another support sometimes used for moribana arrangements consists of interlocking circles into which branches can be fitted. This is useful for heavy material, but not as easy to master as a kenzan. Combined shippo/kenzan are available.

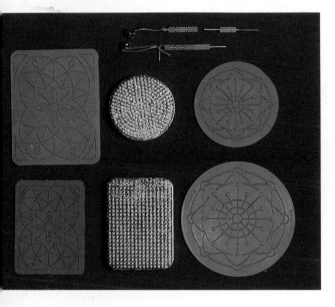

Below *Kenzans with Kenzan mats and Kenzan Naoshi* Round and rectangular mats to go underneath a kenzan; kenzan naoshi showing end unscrewed.

Above right *Hasami: Tsurute & Warabi with case & cap* From left: three sizes of tsurute with hasami case below; warabi and scissor cap.

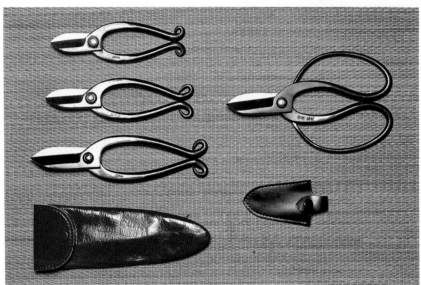

■ KENZAN MATS

Small round and rectangular rubber mats fit underneath the kenzan and prevent it from marking the container are recommended. You can cut your own from foam rubber, but the mats are cheap and durable.

■ CARE OF KENZAN

A good kenzan should last for years. After use scrub with a clean stiff brush, rinse and store upside-down when dry. If the needles get bent or if dirt gets caught in between the needles, use a *kenzan-naoshi*.

■ KENZAN-NAOSHI

This is a simple and practical tool for cleaning and repairing kenzans. It consists of a small, hollow brass rod with a bell attached to help you find it. The head of the rod unscrews, enabling it to be used in two ways: to straighten bent needles and to clean the kenzan.

■ HASAMI: IKEBANA SCISSORS

Hasami are the serious ikebana practitioner's most valuable item. Like a *sushi* chef's knife, it is their one indispensable tool.

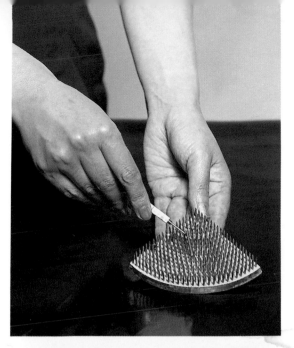

If you are serious about ikebana, sooner or later you will want your own hasami. They do all the cutting you need; thick branches, thin stems, delicate leaves and petals. This well repays their initial cost. Their simplicity and elegance make them a pleasure to handle and, unless misused, they should last for years.

Two styles are available: *warabi*, which have looped handles like Western scissors, and the more widely available *tsurute* (illustrated in this book). Try out both and choose the one that suits you.

Hasami come in different sizes. Try them out, feel their weight and decide which feels more comfortable in your hand.

■ CARE OF HASAMI

Hasami need little care. Wipe them clean and dry them after use. Rub now and then with an oily rag. Properly used they should not need sharpening, but it is possible to sharpen them on a carborundum steel. Although they will not be as good as new after sharpening, they will serve as a useful second pair.

Two words of warning: *Never* twist the blades when cutting – a sure way to blunt the edge. And never use them to cut wire. It will damage the blades irrevocably.

■ HASAMI CASE AND CAP

Some hasami come with their own case. If not, you can get a leather case or little cap to fit over the tips of the blades. This protects them from damage if dropped and also protects your pocket or the bag you carry them in, so is well worth the small outlay of money.

■ SAWS AND KNIVES

Large saws are used for cutting branches and small saws for wedging, an advanced technique beyond the scope of this book. Like all Japanese saws, these cut as you draw the blade toward you, not on the outward stroke, as with Western saws.

The sheathed knife is for paring the ends of branches and making incisions in the bark, not an essential purchase for beginners.

■ MISTER/PUMP

The combination mister/pump is used for spraying material to keep it fresh while you are working, as well as for spraying the finished arrangement. When the nozzle is removed, it can be used to pump water into stems with a high water content, such as water lilies. These sometimes lose their turgidity and go limp. When the water content is restored, they stand upright again.

■ OTHER USEFUL ITEMS

Wire, raffia, rubber bands, string and gutta-percha are handy for fixing, tying, securing and shaping material. You will need a small pair

Above top Bits of stem and dirt often get trapped between the needles. These should be removed or they will make the water smell. Unscrew and reverse the naoshi to expose the pin, and then use it to remove the dirt and clean in between the needles. A toothpick will also do the job fairly well.

Above *To straighten bent needles and to clean the kenzan* Thick branches can bend the kenzan needles. To straighten, slip the hollow end of the naoshi over the bent needle and gently pull upright. The needle should then be tapped lightly with a hammer or heavy object to secure it back in the base.

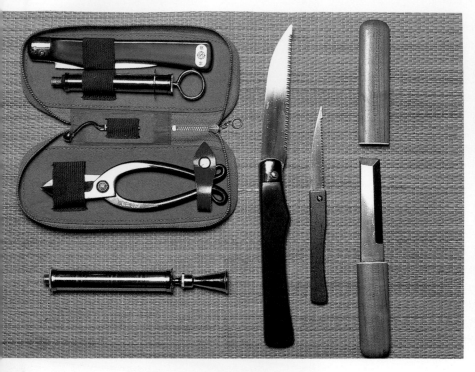

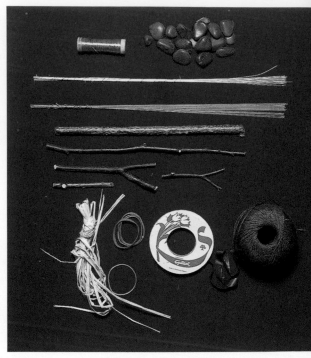

Above *Other Tools*
From left: tool case with saw, mist sprayer, naoshi and hasami; below, mist sprayer; large and small saws opened out; knife and wooden sheath.

Above right From top: reel of wire; pebbles, lengths of wire; straight and forked sticks for kubari; raffia, rubber bands, gutta-percha, string.

of pliers and wire-cutters when using wire. Collect a supply of straight and forked sticks for making *kubari* (supports) for nageire arrangements. Pebbles are sometimes used to cover the kenzan, especially in arrangements using pond and waterside plants.

■ CONTAINERS FOR IKEBANA

The container forms an integral part of the design of an ikebana arrangement in a way that is not always true in Western flower arrangement, in which the vase is subordinate to and sometimes completely hidden by flowers. As much care and thought goes into choosing the container, considering its sympathy with the setting, its aptness for the occasion and how well it suits the material, as into selecting the material itself. Therefore the subject needs discussion.

Classical ikebana arrangements are *shin* (formal), *gyo* (semiformal) or *so* (informal). Classical containers and the materials they are made from are similarly classified.

Formal containers derive their form from classical Chinese shapes and are made of bronze, lacquer or highly glazed ceramic ware. Nowadays glass is sometimes used.

Semiformal and informal containers may be of bamboo, unglazed or matt-glazed ceramic, wood or natural objects like gourds. Baskets are popular as informal containers. In general plain, darker colours and undecorated surfaces are preferred to multicoloured, patterned ones, so that they do not compete with the material and are therefore much easier to work with.

Modern containers are another matter. There is no division into formal and informal. Instead there are moribana (shallow, flat-bottomed), nageire (tall cylindrical, square or bottle-shaped) and free-style (infinitely varied) containers. In Japan fresh collections of containers appear each year, rather like the new season's fashion collections. Different materials like glass, metal and plastic, and fresh colours and shapes are constantly experimented with. Also, objects designed for one perhaps unrelated purpose are adapted to serve as containers for ikebana.

| **Below** *A selection of free-style containers* From left: Funnelled log-shaped vase by Ian Auld; black compote on tall leg decorated with fine incised lines; rounded pot on three legs with streaky glaze and three openings; linked double nageire vase; leaf-shaped moribana vase; turquoise compote with curved lip on a low base.

| **Left above** *A selection of ikebana containers* From left: small standing or hanging basket; bamboo cylinder for seika and nageire styles; square black moribana container; lacquered basket with handle on a kadai; low dish with contrasting glaze inside; antique *sake* bottle; small long-necked bottle.

| **Left below** *A selection of moribana containers* From left: white trough with black lines, raised on two low legs; basic round blue container; half-circle in purple plastic; large black rectangle; oval blue dish.

Above The most basic containers: on the left one for moribana, and on the right one for nageire.

■ STARTING A COLLECTION OF CONTAINERS

The first container you will need is a shallow ceramic one for moribana. This should be round or rectangular, 8–12in/20–30cm across and about 2–2½in/5–6.3cm deep. Oval and semicircular shapes are also suitable. The container must have a flat bottom so that the kenzan can be placed in different positions.

The easiest colours are black, dark brown or dark blue, as all material goes with these colours, and the container itself will then blend in with the setting you have chosen more readily. (There will be quite enough to think about without having to worry about the colour of the container.)

When you come to do nageire you will need a strong cylindrical ceramic vase about 10in/25cm tall and 3½in/9cm in diameter. Some nageire vases have a ridged or roughened band inside, below the lip. This makes it easier to fix the kubari and support the material. Some kubari exert considerable pressure on the sides of the container as the material thus balanced can be fairly heavy, so cheap machine-made ceramic vases that are liable to crack should be avoided. High-fired stoneware is a good choice as it is strong and also heavy enough to be stable. Glass is not a good choice because it shows the fixing and might crack under pressure.

Once you have been doing ikebana for a while you will no doubt want to expand your collection and look for challenging and interesting containers for freestyle and other work. Apart from containers specifically made for ikebana, interior decoration stores, antiques shops, junk stalls and flea markets may be scoured for suitable vases. You may even find yourself joining a pottery class and making your own containers. Using a container of your own design and making is a most satisfying experience.

■ KADAI

A *kadai* is a base placed beneath the container both to protect the surface it stands on and to give dignity and emphasis to the arrangement. Kadai are more often used with classical and traditional arrangements and are obligatory with formal styles, but may be used with modern arrangements too. The simplest is the *shiki-ita*, a regular or irregular wooden shape, polished, painted or lacquered, or an informal bamboo raft. A *maki-ashi* (bent leg style) has ends that scroll under to support it. More elaborate kadai, often intricately carved, may be used with rikka and seika styles. The most common colours are black, dark brown or *shu*, a warm, glowing red.

It is easy to make a simple kadai either from a round sliced off a seasoned log, sanded and possibly stained, or from a smooth, flat piece of wood, stained and given several coats of varnish for a durable and high-gloss finish.

■ SKILLS AND TECHNIQUES

Ikebana involves three basic techniques. These are:

■ cutting, using hasami and other tools

■ shaping the material

■ fixing the branches and flowers securely

Note: The instructions in this chapter are, on the whole, guidelines to help you achieve results rather than hard and fast rules. As you gain experience, you will find out what works for you and no doubt adopt or adapt them to suit yourself, your material and your equipment.

■ CUTTING AND USING HASAMI

There are two kinds of hasami; warabi, and the more widely available and commonly used tsurute, explained in the previous chapter. Tsurute have been used to illustrate cutting techniques in this book.

The first thing is to get used to the feel of your hasami. Hold them, handle them, feel their weight in your hand and practise cutting all kinds of material with them. Being familiar with scissors having looped handles, Westerners are accustomed to using the thumb in the top loop to open and the third finger in the bottom loop to close them. To open and close hasami you need a different action. The arm should be relaxed and free of tension all the way to the shoulder and neck. Practise this movement until you can do it easily.

You will notice that hasami open and close much more freely than ordinary scissors. On examination you will find a small gap between the blades. This can be widened by placing the little finger between the end of the handles. You do this when cutting thick branches. To narrow the gap place your forefinger between the handles. As you straighten it the pressure brings the blades together, making it easier to cut leaves, petals and other fine material.

■ GENERAL TIPS ABOUT CUTTING

■ When cutting, hold the part you intend to use, *not* the part you are cutting off. This eliminates the risk of its falling and getting damaged.

■ Cut stems under water to avoid an airlock. This stops water reaching the leaves and flowers and they droop. Work with a bowl of water nearby for this purpose.

■ The general rule is to cut stems, particularly branches, diagonally. This provides a larger surface for the absorption of water and makes fixing on to the kenzan easier. The exceptions are thin stems like grasses and freesias, or fleshy stems like those of daffodils and amaryllis. These are usually cut straight across. (See section on *Using a Kenzan*)

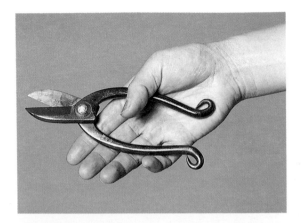

Above top To open hasami the upper handle is held between the thumb and the palm of the hand. The lower handle, allowed to drop freely, is supported by the fingers.

Above To close the hasami, curl the fingers around the lower handle to raise it and bring the blades together. This makes a satisfying percussion sound.

Far right Cutting stems under water lengthens their vase life. **Right** Cutting thicker branches: woody stems like privet, camellia or pine are more of a challenge.

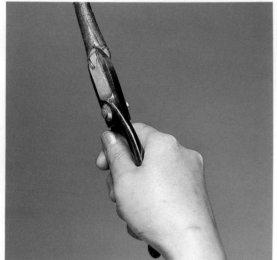

Above Hold the branch with the cut side uppermost. Split it vertically down the centre with the tips of the blades.

■ CUTTING FLOWERS AND THIN STEMS

Flowers should be cut under water. Hold the stem above the point you want to cut, place the stem midway between the tip and the axis of the blades and cut cleanly in one movement. Until you are experienced, always cut stems slightly longer than you think you will need them. You may have to reposition them on the kenzan and need to recut the ends. In fact, it is a good idea to cut *all* stems a bit longer than you expect to need. Cutting is irrevocable; once a stem is too short there is little you can do about it.

■ CUTTING THICKER BRANCHES

Open the hasami to their full extent and place the branch diagonally across the mouth with the blades at an angle. Then, keeping your wrist and arm relaxed, bring the blades together. You may not be able to cut right through a thick branch the first time. Open the blades, reposition the branch and repeat the action as many times as necessary. Do not try to cut with the hand and wrist alone. The energy should come from the *hara* (the solar plexus) up through your shoulders and down your arm. To allow this energy to flow freely your back must be straight. It is often easier to cut branches standing up, feet square and firm on the ground. Do not worry if the hasami pinch your finger. It is one of the hazards of ikebana.

■ PREPARING A BRANCH FOR A KENZAN

Thick woody stems often need to be treated before they can be fixed securely on the kenzan. The most common way is to split the end. Experience will teach you which branches, among them forsythia and camellia, split easily and therefore need care. It is best to experiment with odd pieces of branch first.

■ USING A SAW

Large branches may need to be sawn. Ikebana saws, like all Japanese saws, cut on the inward stroke (Western saws, on the other hand, cut on the outward thrust).

■ SHAPING LEAVES AND PETALS

Sometimes you need to cut away part of a damaged leaf or reshape a leaf or petal that is too large. Stiffish leaves like those of camellia present little difficulty, but delicate leaves are more of a challenge. Use your forefinger to reduce the gap between the blades to its minimum, as described above, and cut gently and carefully with the tips of the blades. Practise on discarded leaves first.

■ TRIMMING

All branches and most flowers will need some trimming. Just how much depends on the material, the style, the season – summer arrangements are fuller and leafier, autumn and winter ones sparser and more austere – and your own taste. Study the arrangements in this book and notice how skilful trimming has been used to create space, reveal line and lighten and change the balance of an arrangement. Then practise on unwanted branches and flowers and notice the results.

■ TRIMMING FLOWERS

Generally flowers have at least two-thirds of their leaves removed. Usually these are pinched off with the fingers. Do this tidily, pinching them off at the base to leave a clean finish. Some flowers, like chrysanthemums, have a bract at the base of the leaf. These should be removed as well. Attention to such details is the hallmark of a well-made arrangement.

Left A very thick branch may need to be step-cut before fixing. Split the end and then cut away one side about ½in/ 1.5cm from the bottom so that you have a manageable end that can be fixed easily and securely.

Centre Use tips of scissors to shape or remove damaged parts of leaves or petals.

Right Cut off side branches close to the main stem.

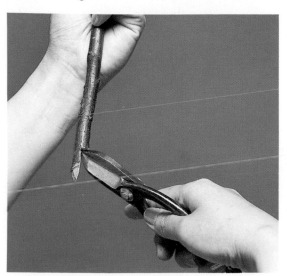

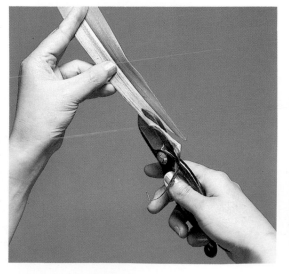

Below Pinching off
leaves

Top left
Chrysanthemum stem
before trimming

Top right The same stem
after trimming

Bottom left Scabious
and love-in-a-mist
before trimming

Bottom right The same
flowers after trimming

■ TRIMMING BRANCHES

When trimming branches your aim is to clarify the line you want to use. First you need to study the branch. All branches have a front and a back, a 'sunny' (*yo*) and a 'shady' (*ur*) side. Learning to recognize this is important.

You also need to notice the movement of the branch. Branches reach upward toward the light and in ikebana all material follows this rule of upward movement. While trimming a branch, hold it as it will go in the arrangement, 'sunny' side tilted toward you and its tip reaching upward.

When you have chosen the line you want to clarify, start to cut away the side branches, checking it repeatedly as you work. Cut off side branches close to the main stem, unless you want to leave a stump for a gnarled and weathered effect. If the resulting fresh scar is conspicuous, rub it with a damp finger and darken it with dirt to blunt the rawness so that it no longer catches the eye.

Where leaves grow symmetrically, remove some to create irregular spaces on the branch. Practise on waste material and note the different effects.

Above The 'sunny' front (left) and 'shady' back (right) of cotoneaster branches

■ MAXIMUM USE OF MATERIAL

Where several flowers grow on one stem, as with spray chrysanthemums, spray carnations and certain lilies, a little forethought can stretch their usefulness and give you many flowers from one stem. The same is true of branches. Keep this in mind when choosing and cutting material.

Do not throw away any material until you have finished. Flowers and side branches cut off your main stems are handy for supporting material and masking the kenzan. Soft thick stems, like those of chrysanthemums and lilies, are useful for 'shoes' to hold a thin stem on a kenzan or to prop up heavy stems. When you start making nageire arrangements you will need woody stems to make kubari, so keep the pieces of branch you cut off.

You will often find that trimmings yield enough material for a smaller arrangement and nearly always for a miniature arrangement as well. Look through trimmings with these in mind.

■ SHAPING YOUR MATERIAL

Sometimes you may be lucky enough to find a branch that is the perfect shape and flowers that face just the way you want them to, but there will be times you need to improve on nature. The techniques described here are not easy to grasp from a book. They need to be practised repeatedly. However, when they are mastered you will find them invaluable. Each material has its own breaking point that can only be learned from experience, so practise on waste material until you come to understand what is possible with the different materials.

Above The same branch trimmed to reveal the chosen line

Below Privet branch before trimming

SHAPING BRANCHES

All branches can be shaped to bend or curve the way you want. However, some materials are more intractable than others. Choose pliable materials like yew, broom or pussy willow to start with.

Before you start, check your position. Sit or stand, back straight, feet square and your weight evenly balanced. Begin by simply holding the branch in your hands and testing its flexibility. Then decide where you want the branch to bend. Avoid the nodes (the areas where leaves, dormant buds or side branches emerge), as these are weak points.

Hold the branch in the direction you want it to go. Make sure the 'sunny' side faces you and the tip reaches up. Put your fingers under the branch so that they touch and make a 'cushion' for the branch. Your thumbs go on top, also touching. Bend gently and feel it responding.

Stop and check how you have altered the shapes. Repeat and study the result until it is bent sufficiently. Try bending a branch to the left and another to the right. With practice your hands will start to understand the character of this material. Next time use a different kind of branch.

Sometimes you will hear a faint cracking sound as you are working. These are the fibres starting to soften and give, rather like your bones and sinews cracking when you stretch in the morning. Don't worry if you break a branch; only then can you learn how far you can go before reaching the breaking point. This not only differs for each kind of material but also depends on season and age (young and old branches, like young and old bones, break more easily).

THICK BRANCHES

If you want to bend a thick intransigent branch, or bend a branch at an angle rather than making it curve, make a slight cut in the bark on what is to become the outer curve. This releases the tension in the bark, and makes it easier to bend to the angle you need. This technique is particularly useful for nageire work.

TWISTING AND BENDING

Pliable material like yew can be twisted as well as bent in order to modify its direction.

ACHIEVING THE RIGHT DIRECTION

Learning how to bend a branch is one thing. Getting it to bend in the way you want is another. Study the branch carefully before you begin. Decide the shape you want to achieve and analyze how to achieve the desired effect. Understanding comes with experience. Practise the skills and study the results. After a while you will find that your hands begin to understand what to do as if by instinct; but this takes time.

Left The four stems on the right have all been cut from a single stem like that on the left

■ SHAPING SOFT STEMS

Flowers require different skills and different techniques are used for moribana and nageire work. Thin branches and stems like freesias and carnations tend to snap easily. Hold the stem lightly between the fingers, one hand near the base and the other below the head, and flex the stem gently. This makes it more pliable and can be used to induce or increase a curve.

With non-fibrous stems that have a high water content (generally monocotyledons whose leaf veins run parallel instead of branching out and forming a network) the technique is to soften the stem by gently stroking at the point at which it is to curve or bend. This technique is used with iris.

Stems of dicotyledonous plants that have a fibrous core, like chrysanthemums, hydrangeas, sweet peas and most lilies (but not arums), are gently stroked and squeezed between the fingers at the point they are to bend. This is mainly used to persuade the flowers to lean forward in a nageire arrangement, in which the bent stem is supported by the rim of the container. The trick is to soften the fibres just enough so that the stem will bend but retain its tension.

Great care must be taken with all these techniques, as it is very easy to break the stems.

Left Fingers touch underneath, making a cushion for the branch

Right Thumbs go together on top and the energy comes from the hara up through the shoulders and down the arms

Left Nicking the branch on on what is to become the outer curve

Right Once the tension in the bark has been released, the branch can be bent at an angle

Left Bent branch resting easily in a jar

Right Shaping a gladioli leaf between the fingers with a swift upward twisting movement

Left Hold the branch in one hand, with your thumb extended along the line of the branch

Right Firmly grasp both branch and thumb with the other hand, then twist and bend at the same time as if you were wringing out a wet cloth

Left Encouraging a thin, springy branch to curve

Right Curved springy branch in jar

Left Stroke and gently squeeze the stem at the point you want it to bend

Right Bent lily with neck supported by rim of vase

Below The branch is pushed straight down on to the kenzan with the cut side opposite the way it will lean

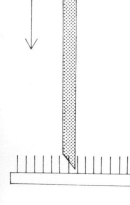

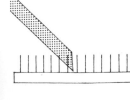

Above The branch is moved into position from the bottom

■ SHAPING LEAVES

The direction of many leaves can be altered by soft stroking or lifting with the fingers. Linear leaves, like those of gladioli, montbretia and iris, are pulled upward between the fingers in one swift, firm, but gentle, twisting movement.

The technique for shaping aspidistra leaves is illustrated with the formal seika arrangement in the Classical Section, under Koryu Arrangements.

All leaves need to be handled with care, especially delicate leaves like those of tulips and daffodils, which rapidly lose their bloom and are weakened if overhandled.

■ FLOWERS AND PETALS

A flower that is still in bud can be encouraged to open by blowing softly onto the petals. These can also be eased open very gently with the fingers. A stunning effect can be achieved with tulips in this way as seen in the floating arrangement (ukibana) using tulips and eucalyptus leaves, in which the flowers have been eased open to suggest water lilies.

At other times a flower, for instance a rose, may have opened too fully. Removing the outer petals will reveal the still unopened centre.

■ FIXING TECHNIQUES

The techniques for securing material for moribana differ from those involved in nageire work. Techniques for nageire are discussed in the step-by-step nageire section. Here we look at how to use a kenzan.

■ USING A KENZAN FOR MORIBANA:
■ BRANCHES

Prepare the branch by cutting the end at an angle. If it is very thick, split it or make a step-end. Hold the kenzan with one hand and with the other grasp the branch firmly near its base. Push the branch straight onto the kenzan. The angled cut faces *away* from the direction the branch is to lean. Make sure it is firmly on the kenzan and then gently move into the correct position from the base. Do *not* move it from the top as this loosens its hold on the kenzan.

The first time you try fixing a branch it is a good idea to put the kenzan on a table, where it is less likely to slip. This is also advisable when fixing thick branches that need a lot of force.

■ FLOWERS

Most flowers are fixed in the same way, ie, pushed straight on the kenzan and then moved into position from the base. They need gentler handling. Soft-stemmed flowers like tulips and daffodils are cut straight; they are best fixed at the required angle to avoid handling more than is absolutely necessary.

■ THIN STEMS

Thin-stemmed flowers might not always be held securely by the needles of the kenzan. In this case, cut a piece from a thicker stem, 1in/2.5cm or less in length. Chrysanthemum off-cuts are the easiest to use. Cut the thin stem at a sharp angle, slip it into the thicker 'shoe' and fix onto the kenzan.

Single grasses can also be fitted with a 'shoe'. If using a bunch of grass, secure the ends with an elastic band and trim before fixing.

Left Fixing a step-cut branch

Right The stem of the rose is supported as it is moved into position

Left Thin chrysanthemum stems fitted with a 'shoe'

Right Heavy-headed gerbera supported with a prop. A second kenzan placed upside-down with the needles interlocking acts as a counterweight to prevent the weight of the flower from overtipping the kenzan

■ HEAVY STEMS AND BRANCHES

You may have difficulty fixing branches and heavy-headed flowers (like gerbera or gladioli) positioned at a low angle, when they tend to collapse under their own weight. Cut a piece from a sturdy, thickish stem to fit on to the kenzan near the bottom of the problem stem and prop it up. Later it can be masked with foliage.

| **Above** Pale gold carnation and eucalyptus stem in ikebana position. Red carnation and eucalyptus in Western position

| **Above right** Iris reaching up in the correct ikebana position. Note the longest stem is a bud, the shortest the most open flower

| **Right** Spider chrysanthemums reaching forward and upward

| **Far right** Full frontal and the outward and downward placement characteristic of Western arrangement

| **Above left** Iris as they would be placed in a Western arrangement | **Above** Showing the correct positioning of cotoneaster branches |

KENZAN AS COUNTERWEIGHT

When using heavy material, particularly low-angled flowers and branches in a slanting or flowing style, the weight may tip up the kenzan. You either need a larger and heavier kenzan or you can use a second kenzan to counterbalance the material. Turn it upside-down and fix it at the back or on the side opposite the direction of the material, so that the needles of the two kenzans interlock.

MASKING THE KENZAN

There is no need to cover the kenzan completely, but it should be masked sufficiently so that it does not distract from the arrangement. This is most effectively done with small pieces of foliage placed so that they reach *forward* on the kenzan. Pebbles can also be used and are especially appropriate in arrangements of waterside material. Dark pebbles are preferable to brightly coloured ones.

GETTING THE RIGHT DIRECTION

In Western flower arrangements, flowers are often placed facing straight on or looking down. In ikebana the material reaches upward toward the sun, following the line of growth. It is important to get this right as it is one of the common mistakes beginners make. Study the examples so that you learn to recognize the subtle difference between the two approaches to the material.

■ GENERAL NOTES

SYMBOLS

The following symbols are used:

●

a circle for Line 1

■

a square for Line 2

▲

a triangle for Line 3

T

T for supporting material

These notes apply to the step-by-step arrangements and the variations that follow. You need to study them before you can understand the instructions for the arrangements. Mark this section so that you can find it easily if you need to refer back to it.

■ THE THREE MAIN LINES

All the basic arrangements and most of the variations use three main lines supported by supplementary material. This applies to both moribana and nageire styles. The lines are given different names by different schools but in all the longest line symbolizes heaven (*ten*), the shortest earth (*chi*) and the intermediary line man (*jin*).

To avoid confusion they are referred to as Lines 1, 2 and 3 in this book and are given symbols as detailed below.

■ LENGTH AND PROPORTION OF LINES

The length of the lines is determined by:
a. the type of material used; thin branches and smaller flowers being left longer, thick, bushy branches and bright or larger flowers sometimes cut shorter than the given measurement.
b. the main factor, ie, the size of the container.

■ THE CONTAINER'S SIZE (C/S)

It is important to get this right, for the balance of your finished arrangement.

Measure the width and the depth of the container.

Add these two measurements to get the measurement known as the container's size (C/S). This is your guide in deciding how long to cut the material.

■ CHOOSING MATERIAL

For your first arrangement choose branches that are not too thick and that have clear lines. Choose flowers with strong stems and single heads so you can concentrate on the design without worrying too much about trimming and other techniques. Advice on material is given later in the book.

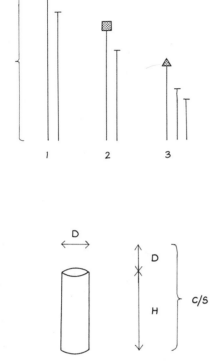

1   2   3

Line 1 (usually a branch) should be between one-and-a-half and two-and-a-half times the C/S depending on the character of the material.

Line 2 (the same material as Line 1) is about three-quarters as long as Line 1.

Line 3 (generally a flower) is one-half to three-quarters the length of Line 2.

Supporting material (either flowers or branches) is shorter and less important that the line it supports. It follows the direction of the line it is supporting.

A

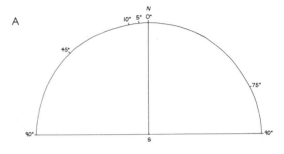

B

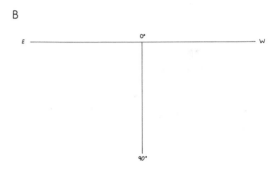

C

Above Measuring the container's size for nageire and moribana containers.

Diagram A shows the position of the three main lines seen from the front. It gives the angles of the lines measured to the right and left of a line 0° drawn vertically through the centre of the kenzan. The branch or stem may curve or bend, but the angle is measured on a line taken from its tip.

Diagram B is a bird's eye view showing the positions of the lines

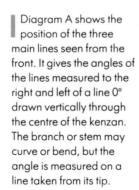

forward, or occasionally backward, from a horizontal line drawn from right to left through the back of the kenzan. The measurement is taken forward or backward from this line 0°, and right or left of a central 90° line.

Diagram C is a close-up of the kenzan showing the point of origin of each of the three lines. Care in placing the branches and flowers correctly on the kenzan helps achieve a neat and pleasing finish.

THE DIAGRAMS

A set of diagrams accompanies each arrangement.
The top diagram shows the position of the three main lines seen from the front. It gives the angles of the lines measured to the right and left of a line 0° drawn vertically through the centre of the kenzan. The branch or stem may curve or bend, but the angle is measured on a line taken from its tip.

■ STEP-BY-STEP MORIBANA ARRANGEMENTS

■ MORIBANA

Moribana is an arrangement made in a shallow container. The name comes from the two words *moru* (to pile up) and *hana* (the term used for branches and flowers). When joined the 'h' is vocalized and pronounced 'b'.

■ EARLY ARRANGEMENTS

The earliest shallow container arrangement was an informal rikka (landscape) style called *sunanomono*, dating from the 16th century. Sunanomono is made in a *sunabachi*: the surface of the vase was covered with a board sprinkled with sand so that the branches and flowers, emerging from an aperture in the covering appeared to be growing in earth. Later, Seika arrangements were sometimes made in shallow containers. Various devices were ingeniously adapted to support the material. Being in themselves attractive, these formed part of the design.

■ MODERN MORIBANA

The moribana style we know today was created around the beginning of this century by Ushin Ohara, founder of the Ohara School. Ohara's moribana was revolutionary in its use of Western flowers and the colourful and highly decorative result rapidly became popular.

■ MORIBANA CONTAINERS

Moribana is made in a shallow container with a flat bottom, which allows the kenzan to be placed in different positions. The container should be between 2–2½in/5–6.5cm deep and 8–12in/20–30cm wide.

The best container for practice would be a black, dark brown or deep blue ceramic one, either round, square or oblong in shape.

■ POSITION OF KENZAN

Generally the kenzan goes on the right or left, depending on whether it is a right- or left-hand version of the style, and either at the front for an upright style, or at the back for a slanting one. The correct kenzan position is important since the 'empty' part of the container balances the arrangement.

The kenzan may move while you are working; check its position when you have finished and correct it if necessary.

Left A sunanomono arrangement against a screen.

■ WATER IN MORIBANA

Water is an integral part of a moribana arrangement. In warm weather the kenzan goes at the back and the water reaches to the brim. The material leans forward and is reflected in the water.

■ MORIBANA PRACTICE

Moribana is easier to master than nageire. It also fits more easily into a Western home and offers many variations.

We will study two basic moribana styles, the Upright and the Slanting, and two versions of each, one designed to go on the left, the other on the right of its setting in their right- and left-hand versions. The arrangements shown, based on the teachings of the Sogetsu School, embody the fundamental principles of ikebana. Practising them will help you grasp and internalize the characteristics of Japanese aesthetics. When you feel confident about these, try the variations that follow.

■ FIRST PRACTICE

This arrangement brings a welcome touch of warmth. The glowing berries and golden hearts of the small chrysanthemum flowers make a cheerful combination for an autumn afternoon, when the days are starting to draw in.

Note: Instructions given for this arrangement are not repeated in the same detail for subsequent practices. It is assumed the reader will either internalize and transfer them or, if necessary, refer back to these pages.

■ MORIBANA BASIC UPRIGHT STYLE

LEFT-HAND VERSION

Every style has a right- and a left-hand version. This left-hand version of the Basic Upright style is designed for table height to go on the left side of a table or in the left corner of a room. Adjustments may need to be made if it is placed higher or lower than table height 27–30in/ 69–76cm. First, gather your equipment and material. You will need:

EQUIPMENT

■ a flat-bottomed moribana container 8–10in/20–25cm wide
■ a kenzan about 3½in/9cm in diameter
■ hasami; or a pair of scissors *and* some secateurs
■ a bowl of water

MATERIAL

■ for Lines 1 and 2: at least two branches, two to two-and-a-half times your container's size
■ for Line 3 (and supporting material); three single flowers (carnations, roses, iris) or one or two stems of spray chrysanthemums
■ for masking the kenzan: any suitable foliage

Below *Ready to start:* the equipment necessary for the first moribana practice.

Below right Diagrams showing the angles of the lines in a left-hand version of the Basic Upright style.

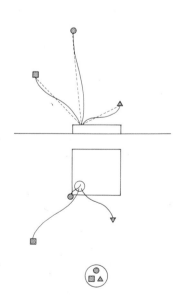

Right
Used in the example: square black ceramic container with early autumn material
▌ Lines 1 and 2 – *Cotoneaster* 'Cornubia'
▌ Line 3 and supporting material – small yellow-centred pompon spray chrysanthemums
▌ for masking the kenzan – *Arachnoides adiantiformis* (leather-leaf fern)

STEP ONE

Measure your container and add its width and depth to find the container's size. Choose the longest and strongest branch for Line 1. Study the branch, decide which is the front, then measure and mark a point between one-and-a-half and two times the container's size. Hold the branch facing you with the tip pointing up and slightly leftward and cut the bottom at an angle in the bowl of water. If the branch is thick, split the end. Remove leaves and side branches to leave a clear 2in/5cm at the bottom and do any preliminary trimming.

Place the kenzan in Position 1 (front left). With the branch still facing you check that the cut side faces right, and push it straight down between the needles of the kenzan, centre-back. Hold the kenzan with one hand to prevent it from slipping and gently ease the base of the branch left and forward until its tip is 5° to 10° left of the vertical and 5° to 10° forward. Stand back about a yard from the arrangement to check this.

STEP TWO

Take your Line 2 branch, hold it upside-down against the first one and mark a point three-quarters from its tip. Now turn the branch right way up, holding it facing you with its tip pointing up and toward your left shoulder. Then cut it on the cross (under water) at the place you have marked. Remove the lower leaves and do any preliminary trimming needed.

This branch goes on the kenzan left-front. Push it straight down with the cut side facing right and the branch facing you. Then move it forward and to the left until the tip is about 45° left of the vertical and forward from the kenzan. When you stand about a yard or a metre away it should reach forward and up toward your left shoulder.

STEP THREE

Choose the least open of your flowers for Line 3. Hold it upside-down to measure it against your second branch and cut it (in the bowl of water) ½ to ¾ as long. Remove the lower leaves and any others you want to. Fix this flower on the right-front of the kenzan and move it gently into position. The tip leans 75° to the right of the vertical and 75° forward from the kenzan.

Check the movement and angles of all three lines. Stand about a yard away with your work on a table in front of you. All the material should reach outward and upward toward you; Line 1 coming from the left to a point above your head; Line 2 to the top of your left shoulder, and Line 3 to just below the top of your right arm. You should feel that *you* are the focal point of the arrangement. Do not continue until you can feel this. You will not succeed unless the movement of the lines is correct at this stage. Look at the arrangement from the side to check the forward movement.

1

2

STEP FOUR

Add one or two flowers to support Line 3. Cut them shorter than the first flower, place them on the kenzan inside the triangle formed by the three main stems and ease them into position to follow the movement of the first flower. If you feel either of the branches need support add smaller branches, but be careful *not* to fill up the spaces in between the lines. This space is an integral part of the composition.

Now add small branches and foliage to mask the kenzan. This is more effectively achieved if you place them leaning forward. You do not need to cover the kenzan completely, you simply need to ensure that it is not obvious.

Tidy up so that you can view the arrangement without a distracting muddle around it. Check that the kenzan is still in the right position and do any final trimming.

Before adding water make sure the container is clean and free of debris that may have fallen into it.

Note: Initially it is easier to work without water in the container but, when you are more experienced, you should put a little water in the container to start with and top it up after the arrangement is placed in position.

3/4

Once the arrangement is complete, it is important to check the side view (**left**) and the bird's eye view (**right**).

■ LEFT-HAND VERSION
FURTHER EXAMPLE

Round blue ceramic container
▮ Lines 1 and 2 – pink gladioli
▮ Line 3 – pale pink double spray chrysanthemum
▮ Supporting material – alstroemeria and leatherleaf fern

This shows how a totally different mood can be achieved by making the same style with different material. In this feminine arrangement, the dramatic straight lines of the gladioli, with their delicately shaded pink flowers, contrast with the soft round shapes of the pale pink chrysanthemums and deeper tones and fluid forms of the alstroemeria.

A note on gladioli: It is not always easy to find good branches for ikebana so it is worth remembering that gladioli, which are available in the shops for much of the year, serve very well for Lines 1 and 2. Pinching out the topmost bud encourages all the lower flowers to open.

■ SECOND PRACTICE

The light, bright foliage of golden privet, the cool mauve of scabious and the pale, delicate blues of love-in-a-mist make this a pleasing combination for the early days of summer, when there is still a touch of freshness in the air. Foliage and side branches have been trimmed for an effect of lightness and airiness.

■ BASIC UPRIGHT
RIGHT-HAND VERSION

Used in the example, square black container and early summer material:
▮ Lines 1 and 2 – *Ligustrum ovalifolium 'Aureo-marginatum'* (golden privet)
▮ Line 3 – *scabious*
▮ Supporting material – *Nigella damascena* (love-in-a-mist) and privet.

This is a mirror image of the first arrangement, so all the instructions are reversed.

Opposite Front and side views of another left-hand version of the Basic Upright style, using different material.

Far left *Step 1* Place the kenzan in Position 2 (right-front). Choose, measure and cut your Line 1 branch. It goes in the centre of the kenzan toward the back, and leans 5° to 10° forward and to the right.

Left *Step 2 and 3* Line 2 goes on the right of the kenzan toward the front and leans forward and about 45° to the right, pointing to your right shoulder. The flower for Line 3 goes on the left front of the kenzan and leans forward and to the left about 75°

Far left *Step 4* Stand back to check the movement of the three lines, remembering to check from the side (left) and above (above) that the material leans forward. Add supporting material and foliage to mask the kenzan. Do final trimming, place in position, adjust if necessary and add water.

4

Right The completed
arrangement. The
material leans forward
from the back left corner
of the container and is
reflected in the water.
A style for hot weather.

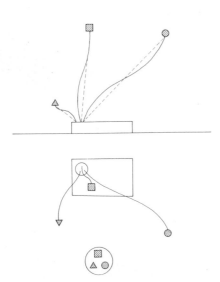

■ THIRD PRACTICE

Dock is such a common weed on roadsides and wasteland that its handsome character and rich colours are often unappreciated. It is easy to work with and its strong lines require little trimming. It lasts well and dries easily, so it is well worth hanging up a bunch or two to dry. Treat with unperfumed CFC-free hairspray to reduce the tendency of dried material to drop off.

Here only white flowers are used so as not to detract from the two predominant colours of russet and golden-green, the green being repeated and intensified in the *Alchemilla mollis* (lady's mantle) that masks the kenzan.

■ BASIC SLANTING STYLE

LEFT-HAND VERSION

Used in the example, black ceramic rectangle with late summer material:

■ Lines 1 and 2 – *Rumex acetosa* (dock)

■ Line 3 – small white pompon bloom chrysanthemum

■ For masking the kenzan – *Alchemilla mollis* (lady's mantle, golden privet

In this style the kenzan is in Position 4 (left-back). Line 1 leans forward across the water at 45° to the right. Line 2 leans in the same direction at 5° to 10°. This means the tops of the two lines are roughly on the same level. Line 3 leans forward to the left 75° from the back.

Step 1 Place the kenzan in Position 4 (left-back). Measure and cut Line 1. Fix on to the kenzan right-front and move into position leaning 45° forward and to the right.

Step 2 Measure and cut Line 2. Fix on to kenzan centre-back and move so that the tip is 5° to 10° to the right and leaning forward. The top should be about the same height as the tip of Line 1.

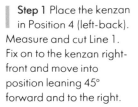

1

Step 3 Measure and cut Line 3 and fix on to the kenzan left-front. Move so that it leans 75° left and forward. Check the three lines.

Step 4 Add supporting flowers and material to mask the kenzan. Place in position, do final trimming, check the kenzan position and, since this is a warm-weather style, top up with water to just below the brim. Check the side view (5).

Above The arrangement viewed from above.

3   5

Below Bird's eye view, showing how the material leans forward.

■ FOURTH PRACTICE
BASIC SLANTING STYLE
RIGHT-HAND VERSION

Gaultheria is a common shrubbery plant, frequently used in parks and civic planting. It has wonderful strong sculptural foliage and this, together with its excellent lasting qualities, makes it ideal ikebana material.

Here the lower leaves have been removed so that the bar stems arch up and those remaining seem to float on air. The pale, deliciously scented creamy roses reach forward from a dense mass of *Alchemilla mollis* (lady's mantle). This arrangement would look well in a low position where the foliage is seen to best advantage.

Used in the example, deep blue ceramic oval vase with summer material:

- Lines 1 and 2 – *Gaultheria shallon*
- Line 3 – pale creamy pink roses
- For masking the kenzan: *Alchemilla mollis* (lady's mantle)

Step 1 Place the kenzan in Position 3 (right-back). Measure and cut the Line 1 branch. This goes on the kenzan left-front and leans forward and to the left at an angle of 45°.

Step 2 Line 2 is fixed on the kenzan centre-back. It leans forward and left 5° to 10°. Its tip should be more or less level with Line 1.

Step 3 Line 3 goes on the kenzan right-front and leans forward and right 75°. Stand back to check the angles and movement of the three lines as seen from the front and the sides.

Right Step 4 Add supporting flowers and material to mask the kenzan. Do final trimming, then place the arrangement in position. Make any adjustments that seem necessary and fill with water to just below the brim.

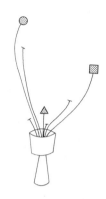

| **Left** Upright style: left-hand version with eucalyptus and pink roses.

| **Below** Upright style: left-hand version with eucalyptus and red carnations.

■ MORIBANA VARIATIONS
ARRANGEMENTS FOR SMALL SPACES
UPRIGHT STYLE: LEFT-HAND VERSION

Used in the example: tall, black ceramic compote decorated with pale gold incised lines; summer material:

▮ Lines 1 and 2 – *Eucalyptus perriniana*

▮ Line 3 – pale pink 'Gerda' roses

This intimate style suits a small space. It is usually made in a compote, or stemmed vase, with the kenzan placed in the centre toward the front. Line 1 is 5° to 10° forward and to the left, as in the Basic Upright style, and Line 2 is 45° forward to the left. The flower for Line 3 reaches straight forward at an angle of 75°, pointing at your heart. The height of the container and the soft yet sophisticated colours of the foliage and flowers give this arrangement a cool elegance and charm.

Used in the example: low square beige compote with summer material:

▮ Lines 1 and 2 – *Eucalyptus perriniana*

▮ Line 3 – red carnations

▮ Filler material – x *Solidaster luteus*

Here the same style is made in a roughly finished, square compote that stands on a low foot. The same material is used for Lines 1 and 2, but the vase and the vivid red carnations that are used for Line 3 change the character of the arrangement, making it bright and friendly. The mass of tiny yellow solidaster used as filler adds to its warm, welcoming air.

| **Opposite** By the
simple device of
placing the material on
separate kenzan, on
opposite sides of
the container, a more
imposing effect
is achieved.

■ ARRANGEMENT WITH ONLY TWO LINES

UPRIGHT STYLE: LEFT-HAND VERSION

Used in the example: low, square stone-coloured compote with flowers available spring through to autumn:

■ Line 1 – two stems of red gladioli
■ Line 3 – one stem of white spider spray chrysanthemum
■ Supporting material – one leaf of *Fatsia Japonica*

This compact style suits a narrow space and uses very little material. The gladiolus used for Line 1 leans forward and slightly to the left. The tip curves in and reaches up. A second supporting gladiolus with more open flowers is placed in front of it. The spider chrysanthemum has been cut to give several flowers from one stem. The half-open bud used for Line 3 leans forward and to the right at an angle of 45°, with shorter and more fully open flowers supporting it and Line 1. The bright resonant green of the palmate fatsia leaf accents and sets off the pale creamy chrysanthemum flowers and contrasts with the darker matt green of their leaves.

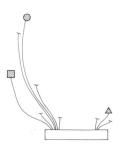

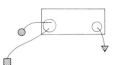

■ A DIVIDED ARRANGEMENT

UPRIGHT STYLE: LEFT-HAND VERSION

Used in the example: black rectangular container with late summer material

■ Lines 1 and 2 – *Rosmarinus officinalis* (common rosemary)

■ Line 3 – pale gold carnations

■ Supporting material – white spider spray chrysanthemum, carnations, rosemary and erica (heather)

This is essentially the Basic Upright style we have seen before, but now divided on 2 kenzans. Branches of common rosemary are used for Lines 1 and 2. These go on a kenzan in the left-front of the container while Line 3, a pale gold carnation, is on a smaller kenzan at the right-front. Rosemary, creamy spider chrysanthemums and additional carnations serve as supporting material, with heather to mask the kenzans. The result is an arrangement that feels considerably larger and richer. The colours used here are subtle ones but stronger hues would make a dramatic impact.

A similar treatment may be applied to make a divided version of the Basic Slanting style, and of course, of the right-hand versions of both styles.

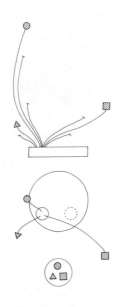

■ AN ARRANGEMENT WHERE ONE LINE LEANS BACKWARD

UPRIGHT STYLE: LEFT-HAND VERSION

Used in the example: round blue container with Mediterranean or Australian material:

■ Line 1 and 2 – *Callistemon citrinus* (bottlebrush)

■ Line 3 – yellow roses

■ Supporting material – acacia (mimosa) and sugar-bush foliage

Bottlebrush, with its neat foliage and elegantly curving branches, is good ikebana material. Here it is used for Line 1, which leans backward to the left at 10° to 15°, and for Line 2, which leans forward to the right at 45° so that, seen from above, the two branches together form a diagonal line across the container. The yellow rosebud for Line 3 leans forward and left at 75°. More open buds support it, while feathery honey-scented mimosa supports Lines 1 and 2. Short stems of bright yellow-green sugar-bush mask the kenzan. The kenzan is in Position 1, but, since the Lines are so evenly spaced, the arrangement looks equally good with the kenzan in Position 2 (right-front).

Right The sweeping main branch of this arrangement reaches backwards, making the arrangement attractive when seen from the side (above) as well as from the front.

■ ARRANGEMENTS FOR LARGER SPACES

UPRIGHT STYLE: LEFT-HAND VERSION

Used in the example: large blue oval container with late summer material:

■ Lines 1 and 2 – *serrata*

■ Line 3 – magenta spray chrysanthemum

■ Supporting material – pale pink single spray chrysanthemum, with spoon-shaped petals *Liatris spicata*

Kenzan Position 1.

In this arrangement Line 1 is in the same position as for the Basic Upright style (5° to 10° forward and left) while Lines 2 and 3 have exchanged positions. Line 2 is 75° forward and to the right. The branches used for Lines 1 and 2 have been trimmed to show the interesting angle of Line 1, the shape of the leaves and to create varied spaces between the foliage. Both are supported by dramatic stems of purple liaris.

The dense magenta chrysanthemums used for Line 3 lean forward and 45° to the left. They are supported and set off by delicate pale pink chrysanthemums. Because of the wide space betwen Lines 1 and 2, this arrangement can dominate a large space. It is therefore a good style to use for a table in a large hall on the left (or in its opposite right-hand version, on the right) of a speaker. Being so powerful it needs a space between it and its viewers.

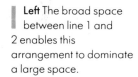

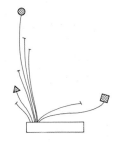
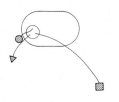

■ **Left** The broad space between line 1 and 2 enables this arrangement to dominate a large space.

■ **Above** The arrangement seen from the side.

ARRANGEMENTS FOR A DINNER TABLE

Ikebena table arrangements use more flowers in relation to their size and, since they are to be seen from all sides, tend to be fuller than other styles. However, they still follow the principles of assymetric balance, incorporation of space and upward movement of the material. Certain points, applicable to all table arrangements, must be remembered:

▪ Since food is the most important element at a meal, flowers should be subordinate and should complement the colours in the dishes.

▪ The flowers should not be too strongly scented or too bright.

▪ The arrangement should be low enough for guests on opposite sides of the table to be able to see one another and converse comfortably.

▪ The guests' first view is before they sit down. This must be checked as well as the all-round view. When working, turn the arrangement to see it from all sides, then stand up to view it from above.

▪ Since the flowers are seen close up and subject to close attention during lapses in conversation and intervals between courses, you must be scrupulous about masking the kenzan. It is also important to make sure the foliage is clean, so remove any damaged or unsightly leaves.

TABLE ARRANGEMENT IN A SHELL-SHAPED VASE USING YELLOW ROSES

This began as an *isshu-ike*, or arrangement using only one type of material, in this case, yellow roses. But then it was felt something was needed to lighten the density of the rose leaves and so *Animi majus* (Queen Anne's Lace) was added, which also helped to mask the kenzan.

Roses, which are lovely in profile as well as when seen full on, are a good choice for a table arrangement. These follow the curve of the shell-shaped vase. The tallest flower reaches forward eagerly from one side with two slightly shorter flowers supporting it. Three lower flowers, still following this movement, fill out the arrangement. A single bud reaching in the opposite direction balances and stabilizes the composition.

■ TABLE ARRANGEMENT IN A DIAMOND-SHAPED VASE

This is a sparkling arrangement that uses charming little daisylike spray chrysanthemum flanked by deep pink spray carnations. The delicate foliage of *Spiraea X arguta* reaches upward and outward in lovely natural lines and gives the whole composition a lovely lightness.

■ TABLE ARRANGEMENT IN A HEXAGONAL PLASTIC VASE

Flowers that had been saved from larger arrangements were used to make this low arrangement in varying shades of yellow. A touch of contrasting purple sets off the yellows. The long spray of bottlebrush on one side extends the horizontal line and provides the asymmetric balance. Flowers include spray carnations, various small-spray chrysanthemums and freesia.

Above Table arrangement in a diamond-shaped bamboo vase.

Left Table arrangement in a shell-shaped vase using yellow roses.

■ *MORIMONO:* ARRANGEMENTS WITH FRUIT AND VEGETABLES

If you have no flowers in the house, why not try an arrangement with fruit or vegetables? This is another arrangement that can be made very quickly at the last minute using a dark shallow plate, glass dish, small grass mat or wooden bowl. The fruit and vegetables should be chosen and grouped for variety of texture, colour and shape, and between one- and two-thirds of the container should be left bare. Check that the arrangement is interesting and attractive from all sides and remember also to view it from above.

Right Yellow and green peppers gleam voluptuously beneath the dry and papery husk of a corn cob. Three humble Brussels sprouts introduce a further contrast in texture and colour tone, while a single leek rises across them in a dynamic line and falls away elegantly on the farther side.

Above The richly patinated surface of this wooden African platter makes a handsome foil for the acid yellow of the lemons which are set at one end against the soft green pile of grapes and decorated with small sprigs of red berries. A single mandarin orange gleams at the other end, with two tiny yellow-eyed chrysanthemums nestling against its flank.

Left A substantial piece of ginger forms the foundation of this composition and anchors the two sprays of cotoneaster that arch across and extend it well beyond its wooden base.

Above A weightier composition, this arrangement uses berried cotoneaster branches and bright yellow pompon spray chrysanthemums flanked by sprigs of leatherleaf fern.

■ SHIKIBANA: LAID FLOWERS

This is something you can do very quickly at the last minute when you have no time to make a proper arrangement. In *shikibana* the flowers and sprays of foliage are laid directly on the table or cloth. The arrangement is made in a moment to last a few hours at most. Since the flowers are not in water it is important to choose material that will survive the evening and will not wilt. A surprising number will last: you can safely use carnations, chrysanthemums, camellias, lilies, orchids, gladioli and freesias.

Lay the foliage first and place the flowers off-centre. Make sure that it looks attractive from all sides and take caré to hide the cut ends of branches, flower stems and foliage.

Your guests may be tempted to play with your arrangement. No matter; you can get them to recompose it and share the pleasure you had in making it.

Left Sprays of bottlebrush run in flowing lines from the single pale pink alstroemeria at the heart of this graceful shikibana.

Left This single scarlet carnation against dark, shiny camellia leaves, laid on a crocheted mat, with a spray of pine needles and a cluster of white berries, would add a seasonal note to a Christmas table.

■ UKIBANA: FLOATING FLOWERS

On a hot summer day or sultry night, flowers floating on a bowl of water introduce a delicious note of coolness. Choose open-faced flowers with water-resistant petals that will not rot quickly. Water lilies are ideal, but others like chrysanthemums, carnations, camellias, dahlias, gladioli and sunflowers can be used as well. Foliage should not be forgotten either.

Fill a low shallow dish or bowl with water, place a small kenzan in one corner to anchor the material, or simply float flowers freely on the surface. Leave about two-thirds of the surface of the water clear. The dish should be placed low down on a table or even on the floor. A bowl with a flower or two floating in it at the entrance or half-way up the stairs is a pleasant greeting for guests or for you.

Opposite This is the simplest kind of floating arrangement. One large yellow-centred chrysanthemum floats freely in a square black dish with three small companions.

Above In this delightful arrangement pale pink tulips have been eased open to simulate water lilies. Round *Eucalyptus perriniana* leaves, reminiscent of water lily pads, float around them, strengthening the allusion.

Right A single red carnation rests in a clear glass bowl against a trimmed *Fatsia japonica* leaf. Random stems of grass float below the water.

| **Above** Two moribana arrangements, Basic Upright in a square container and a Basic Slanting in a rectangular container, are combined to make a large spreading display.

■ COMBINATION ARRANGEMENTS

BASIC UPRIGHT LEFT &
BASIC SLANTING RIGHT

Used in the example early autumn material:

Basic Upright arrangement – square black container

▮ Lines 1 and 2 – *Cotoneaster* 'Cornubia'

▮ Line 3 – small, yellow-centred spray chrysanthemums

▮ For masking the kenzan – leatherleaf fern

Basic Slanting – rectangular black container

▮ Lines 1 and 2 – *Ligustrum ovalifolium 'Aureovariegatum'* (variegated privet)

▮ Line 3 – rust-coloured single-flowered spray chrysanthemums

By the simple device of combining two complementary styles and using harmonizing material, you can make a large and effective display for a party, reception or other function. Experiment with combinations of different styles by placing them in different relationships to each other. Upright and Slanting moribana together, as shown here, is an obvious choice. Place the two arrangements further apart to occupy a larger space.

The combination of the left-hand version of the Upright style with the right-hand version of the Slanting style, where the lines move inward toward each other, contains the arrangement within its parameters. If a *left* version of the Slanting arrangement is used instead, the arrangement reaches outward across the space to its right.

Left Here the Basic Upright moribana arrangement used opposite is combined with a nageire version of the same style, for a space with a higher ceiling.

■ COMBINATION ARRANGEMENT

MORIBANA AND NAGEIRE

BASIC UPRIGHT LEFT

Used in the example: autumn material

Moribana arrangement in square black container

- Lines 1 and 2 – *Cotoneaster* 'Cornubia'
- Line 3 - yellow-centred pompon spray chrysanthemum
- For masking the kenzan – leatherleaf fern

Nageire arrangement in tenmoku cylinder vase

- Lines 1 and 2 – *Cotoneaster* 'Cornubia'
- Line 3 – yellow pompon spray chrysanthemum
- Filler – *Ligustrum ovalifolium 'Aureovariegata'* (variegated privet)

Here two Basic Upright arrangements using very similar material, one moribana and the other nageire, are placed a little apart to make one composition. Although the position of the lines is similar and the containers simple in form, the contrast between the tall and low arrangements adds interest. The branches and flowers repeat themselves like variations on a musical theme played in different keys.

■ NAGEIRE

Nageire is a natural, informal style dating from the 16th century. It is usually made in a tall, cylindrical vase.

■ ORIGINS OF NAGEIRE

Nageire literally means 'thrown in'. The first magazine arrangement is attributed to the great tea-master, Sen-no-Rikkyu who often accompanied the military leader, Hideyoshi, on campaigns so that he could relax after a day on the battlefield and regain a sense of calm while enjoying the ritual of the tea ceremony. Once, when no vase was available, Rikkyu cut a length of bamboo and, tying a few flowers to a sword, tossed them into the improvised container. The result greatly pleased Hideyoshi, who exclaimed with delight at this 'thrown-in' style; the name, nageire, stuck. However, flowers simply 'thrown in' seldom please, and this seemingly 'artless art' requires a high degree of skill.

■ NAGEIRE CONTAINERS

The best vase for initial practice is a simple cylinder 10–12in/25–30cm tall and 3–4in/7.6–10cm in diameter. Nageire can also be made in a tall vase that curves in at the mouth, or in a bottle-shaped vase.

Bamboo is a classic material for nageire vases. Containers of plain or lacquered wood lined with copper are also suitable, as are stoneware ceramic containers. Glass and lightweight machine-made ceramic vases are best avoided, since they are liable to crack under pressure. Clear glass is also unsuitable as it reveals the mechanics and thus detracts from the arrangement.

■ BALANCE AND TRIMMING

Since in a nageire arrangement you are using various techniques to balance the branches and flowers, rather than supporting them on a kenzan as in moribana, major trimming should be done before attempting to place and fix the flowers and branches. More time needs to be spent studying the branches, testing their weight and shaping them. With forethought and skill you can often correct a branch that persists in swinging round from the required position, so that it balances easily. This is done by judicious trimming of leaves and side branches that weigh it in the wrong direction and by bending the branch to alter its shape, as described in the section on skills and techniques.

■ FIXING TECHNIQUES FOR NAGEIRE

Supports for nageire arrangements are called *kubari* and can be made from straight or forked sticks of varying thicknesses.

| **Above** From left Elegant, curved pale turquoise vase, ridged dark blue vase, basic cylinder with *tenmoku* glaze; vase suitable for chabana; cylindrical vase with speckled oatmeal glaze.

| **Opposite, top** Ju-ji cross and Y-shaped kubari in place seen from above.

| **Opposite, middle** Whiteleaf branch to be used for nageire before trimming.

| **Opposite, bottom** The same branch after trimming.

■ THE *JU-JI* CROSS KUBARI

The simplest type, although not always the easiest to control, is a cross made from two pieces of stick inserted securely into the mouth of the container.

To make, take a strong but pliable branch about as thick as your little finger (yew and willow are easy to work with) and cut two pieces from it. Cut each very *slightly* longer than the container's internal diameter, with slightly slanting ends. Holding the first piece at an angle, put it into the container and straighten it as you bring your hand out so that the ends grip the sides of the container. If it is too long you may need to shave a little off one end. When fixed you should be able to lift the container by it. This takes a little practice.

The second piece is fixed in the same way at right angles below the first to make the cross.

■ **Warning:** This fixing should only be attempted in a strong container, since the pressure is likely to crack a glass or machine-made earthenware vase. When working the material should all be placed in *one* of the four sections made by the cross.

■ THE Y-SHAPED KUBARI

In this variation of the ju-ji cross, a forked twig is fixed in the same way as the ju-ji cross. The material is held between the arms of the fork.

■ BALANCING HEAVY BRANCHES

Often a branch swings round from the position you want. If this happens use one of the following supports.

■ THE *SO-EGI-DOME* OR DROP-STICK SUPPORT

This gives firm and flexible support and is especially useful with larger and heavier branches.

Choose a strong stick about as thick as your middle finger and as tall as your container. Pare the top. Hold the branch to be supported in position, cut it to the correct length and split the end vertically. Insert the pared top of the drop-stick into the split branch. The branch will pivot up and down on the drop-stick, allowing you to adjust the angle.

If necessary cut the bottom of the drop-stick so that its top is out of sight and the supported stick below the water level.

One or more drop sticks can be used in the same vase.

■ THE *ICHI-MON-JI-DOME* OR SINGLE-BAR SUPPORT

This is for supporting low-angled branches for a slanting or hanging style.

Take a stick about as thick as your little finger and cut a piece marginally shorter than the container's internal diameter. Holding your

1

2

3

This page

1 Sticks pared for drop-stick supports.

2 Split branch fixed on drop-stick.

3 Branch supported on drop-stick and placed at low angle.

Opposite page

4 Branch supported on drop-stick and placed at high angle.

5 Branch balanced using the drop-stick method.

6 Two drop-sticks used in the same vase.

7 Single-bar support in position in split branch.

8 Branch supported by single-bar and placed at a low angle.

9 Branch supported by single-bar and placed at a higher angle.

10 Iris held in place by a toothpick piercing the stem.

11 Thin supple branch held in place by tension.

12 Iris stem bent and held in place by tension.

branch in position, split the end horizontally. Insert the single-bar into the split end and place in the container with the ends of the bar resting lightly against the sides to balance the branch. The angle can be altered by placing the end of the branch low down or higher up in the container.

▐ **Note:** If the bar is not secure in the split branch, bind the joint with raffia or wire or use an elastic band to strengthen it.

■ SUPPORT BY TENSION

Thin pliable branches and stems can be bent backward or forward so that they are held in place by their own pressure on the side of the container.

■ BEND AND BALANCE

When you have some experience of trimming and bending branches, you will find that sometimes you can dispense with a support altogether. Decide on the direction and angle of the branch and bend it at a point about 2in/5cm from where it will rest on the lip of the vase. Then cut the end at an angle to lie snugly against the container. This is easier with a branch receiving some support from the material already in position.

■ FIXING FLOWERS

Flowers are added after the main branches are in place, so they receive some support from material already in the vase. Decide how the flower is to go and which way it should face. Holding it in position, bend by gently stroking and squeezing the stem 1 or 2in/3 to 5cm below where it will rest on the rim. Be sure to leave it long enough to balance the head. It need not touch the bottom; usually it is angle-cut to rest against the side.

■ PIERCING

Flowers with a thicker stem — iris, lilies and so on — can be pierced with a toothpick. This works in the same way as the single-bar support.

■ SUPPORT BY TENSION

A supple flower stem can be bent back or forward and held in place by its own pressure against the side of the vase in the same way as a pliable branch.

Although the skills and techniques for nageire require patience and practice, you will find the effort of mastering them well worth your while. The greater freedom and subtlety of nageire and its infinite variety make it a most rewarding style.

4

5

6

7

8

9

10

11

12

NAGEIRE STEP-BY-STEP

FIRST PRACTICE
NAGEIRE BASIC UPRIGHT STYLE
LEFT-HAND VERSION

This left-hand version should go on the left of the surface it stands on, if possible against a plain background so that the lines are clearly seen. It can be placed either low or relatively high but needs some space above because of the strong upward movement of the branches. Do not put it where it is likely to be knocked over by people passing in front of it. Its mirror image, the right-hand version, would of course be placed on the right.

Used in this example: cylindrical stoneware vase with deep brown *tenmoku* glaze and autumn material

■ Lines 1 and 2 – *Cotoneaster* 'Cornubia'
■ Line 3 – small yellow pompon spray chrysanthemum
■ Filler – variegated privet and conifer

Method of fixing: Lines 1 and 2 – single-bar support; Line 3 – bending

Step 1 The branch chosen for Line 1 bent naturally and side branches were removed to leave a single clear line. The stem was placed low down in the vase with the branch resting against the rim and its tip 10° to 15° from the vertical on the left and 10° to 15° forward. The visible part is one-and-a-half times the container size.

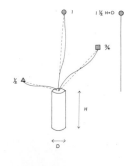

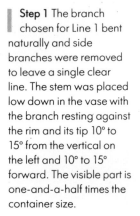

1

Step 2 As neither of the two main divisions of Line 2 gave the right angle, both were left. The lower branch should have been cut shorter. This branch was fixed in the same way as the first in front of the Line 1 branch. The visible part is three-quarters of Line 1 and leans forward left at 45°.

2

3

Step 3 Opposite The chrysanthemum used for Line 3 was bent to lean forward and rest on the rim at 75° to the left. Because the flowers are such a strong yellow the visible length, seen more clearly in the side view, is only one-third that of Line 2.

Step 4 After the lines had been checked flowers were added to fill out the arrangement, together with small sprays of variegated privet and conifer. The completed arrangement was then placed in position and topped up with water.

Above Bird's-eye view showing both the forward and sideward movement of the material.

4

Step 1 A branch that bent naturally was selected and trimmed for Line 1. The branch was cut so that it could rest against the left side about halfway down the vase, and a single-bar support used to balance it. It leans forward to the right at an angle of 45°.

Step 2 The Line 2 branch, also trimmed, rests on the floor of the vase. It leans forward and right at 5°. The stems are appear as a single branch.

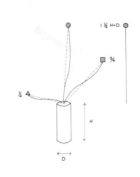

■ SECOND PRACTICE
**NAGEIRE BASIC SLANTING
RIGHT-HAND VERSION**

This arrangement should go on the right with the branches reaching across the surface it rests on. It is a more suitable style for a low-ceilinged room.

Used in this example: cylindrical stoneware vase with speckled, buff-coloured glaze and summer or autumn material.

■ Lines 1 and 2 – rhododendron

■ Line 3 – two single chrysanthemum blooms

■ Filler –*Danae racemosa* (Alexandrian laurel), *Limonium latifolium* (sea lavender)

Method of support: Line 1 – single-bar support; Line 2 – balanced; Line 3 – bent and balanced

1

2

3

Below The side view shows how the material leans forward.

Step 3 The rich golden blooms used for Line 3 lean forward and left at 75°.

Step 4 The completed arrangement. Sprays of *Danae racemosa* were added to fill out the lower part of the arrangement, and a touch of sea lavender softens the blooms.

Above You see both the sideways and forward movement in the bird's eye view.

Top left *Step 1* Line 1 should rise before sweeping forward, left and *down* about two-thirds the height of the container. It should spring up from the mouth, not droop sadly and lifelessly.

Bottom left *Step 2* Line 2 follows the leftward movement of Line 1 but reaches higher and not as far forward. A side branch reaches back, providing depth.

■ THIRD PRACTICE
NAGEIRE HANGING STYLE
LEFT-HAND VERSION

This graceful style is best enjoyed in a relatively high position, perhaps on a mantelpiece. The central placement of the flowers means that it can be set closer to the middle, though not at dead centre.

Note: This is an Ichiyo School style wherein branches are used for all three lines with the flowers placed centrally.

Used in the example: Japanese ceramic nageire vase with streaky turquoise and white glaze and summer material.

■ Lines 1, 2 and 3 – *Jasminum nudiflorum* (winter jasmine)

■ Flowers – deep pink carnations

Method of fixing – bend and balance

1

2

3

Below The side and bird's eye views show the movement of the branches and flowers.

Opposite *Step 3* Line 3 reaches up and then forward and down to the right, so that its tip is roughly level with the rim of the container.

Left *Step 4* The completed arrangement: the first flower is placed in the centre leaning forward, with two flowers added behind it at a slightly higher level to form a triangle and add depth.

4

CLASSICAL IKEBANA

While classical ikebana lies outside the scope of this book, some classical arrangements have been included, for without some idea of its roots, modern ikebana cannot really be appreciated. If from looking at these arrangements you feel that this is the ikebana you want to learn, you should find a teacher to study with.

There are many schools of classical ikebana. Those represented here are the Ikenobo, the oldest school, and the Koryu, which emerged in the 16th century. Like other classical schools, these have developed contemporary styles while continuing to teach the traditional ones.

▌ **Above** classical *usubata* for formal seika on a black-lacquer *maki-ashi* (curved-leg) kadai; bronze *tsuri-tsuki,* moon vase, on a monkey chain; bamboo vase for informal seika on black wooden bases; bronze vase for chabana on a bamboo raft; *niju-ike,* bamboo vase for two-tiered seika on a kadai.

▌ **Above, right** A selection of Japanese baskets for nageire and chabana arrangements. From left: two modern bamboo baskets; fish-trap basket; basket for summer flowers and grasses; twig basket; latticework basket antique lacquered-bamboo basket; modern basket of black bamboo.

■ CONTAINERS

It is not anticipated that you will buy containers like those shown here – even modern replicas are expensive – but the ability to recognize them is helpful. In fact, you should take every opportunity to see Japanese art, either in films or on television, in museums or galleries specializing in Oriental art, at auction sales of Japanese art or, should you be lucky enough to be able to visit Japan, in the country itself. In this way you will develop a feeling for Japanese aesthetics, for its style and use of colour and space, which will greatly benefit your work.

Classical containers, like the arrangements made in them, are shin (formal), gyo (semiformal) and so (informal).

■ IKEBONO ARRANGEMENTS

MODERN RIKKA

Container: modern glass vase with a wide mouth for modern rikka

Material: wisteria vine, montbretia leaves, pink gladioli 'Meyeii', scabious, sword fern (*Nephrolepsis exaltata*), single-flowered pink *Asparagus densiflorus,* hosta leaves

Method of support: kenzan

This elegant arrangement is a very feminine intepretation of the rikka style. The material represents features in a landscape high peak, sunlit slope, shaded valley and so on – but there is no need to understand the symbolism to appreciate the harmony between the lovely arch of the wisteria and the dramatic diagonal sweep of the montbretia leaves, or the graceful positioning of the flowers.

Below More than any other arrangement in the book, this one justifies the claim that ikebana is art.

Right An elegant classical arrangement using a single kind of material, in this case, hydrangeas. This is an Ikenobo shoka style.

■ INFORMAL SHOFUTAI SHŌKA (ISSHU-IKE) ARRANGEMENT

Container: basket made from black bamboo
Material: mauve hydrangeas
Method of fixing: Y-shaped kubari

Shōka is the name used by the Ikenobō School for the style generally known as seika. The stems are arranged and held in the kubari to look as if all the branches spring from a single stem. This is no small achievement requiring patience and skill. Leaves have been trimmed to clarify the springing lines of the central and right-hand branches and the submissive curve of the flower that arches left to balance the design. The overall effect is one of modesty and natural simplicity.

■ SHIMPUTAI

Container: modern ceramic vase based on a classical design
Material: Montbretia leaves, wisteria, 'Stargazer' lily

Shimputai is a modern Ikenobo design derived from the early tate-bana, or standing-flowers, style. In this beautiful arrangement the material rises from the centre of the vase in a single line. The montbretia leaves have been shaped so that they seem to vanish then reappear, as if they had been painted with a fine brush. One leaf leans leftward, balancing the single spray of wisteria on the opposite side. Near the base the open lily expresses the fulfilment of this moment, while the aspiring bud to its left holds promise for tomorrow.

Left The simple beauty of shimputai, a modern Ikenobo style.

■ KORYU ARRANGEMENTS
FORMAL SEIKA
Container: bronze usubata on black-lacquer maki-ashi style base
Material: aspidistra leaves
Method of fixing: Y-shaped kubari
Handsome, darkly gleaming aspidistra leaves are the only material used in this isshu-ike (one material) seika arrangement. The leaves are shaped by being dipped in water, having their tips wound up tightly and then rolled back and forth between the tips of the fingers.

The leaves are first cut and arranged in the hand and then placed between the arms of a Y-shaped kubari inserted into the mouth of the container. A small stick holds them securely.

Below Close-up of aspidistra stems securely held by bar across Y-shaped kubari.

Right This striking and highly stylized seika arrangement takes years to master.

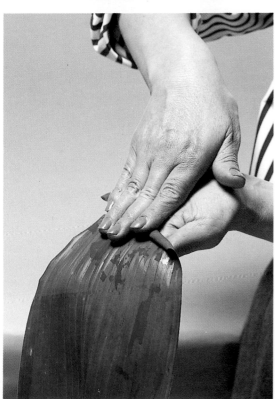

Left To shape aspidistra leaves: first dip the tip of the leaf into water, then having rolled it up tightly, roll back and forth between the fingers to create an elegant curve.

Right The addition of roses brightens and softens the formal lines of this seika arrangement.

■ SEMIFORMAL SEIKA

Container: bamboo vase on brown-lacquer maki-ashi base
Material: golden Irish yew, yellow roses
Method of fixing: Y-shaped kubari

A *nishu-ike* (using two types of material) seika arrangement where yellow roses, picking up the light tones in the golden yew which form the first two lines, are used for the third, or tome, line and supporting material.

■ INFORMAL SEIKA IN MOON VASE

Container: bronze tsuri-tsuki (hanging-moon vase) suspended by a chain of linked monkeys

Material: *Callistemon citrinus* (bottlebrush), small yellow chrysanthemum

With its clear night skies autumn is the best season for moon-viewing. The autumn moon-viewing festival, *jugoya,* is held 15 September. People sit on the veranda, drinking *sake* and watching the moonrise. Offerings of moon-shaped dumplings made from rice flour are piled on a ceremonial stand on the veranda alongside glowing *mikan* (Japanese oranges) and other harvest trophies.

A basket with autumn grasses can be placed nearby and in the tokonoma you can put a *tsuri-bana* (hanging-flower arrangement) in a moon-shaped vase. Early or late in the moon's cycle a crescent-moon vase is used, but at full moon the full circle is appropriate.

The arrangement in the picture is a formal seika style.

Left The relaxed and flowing lines and the simple flowers chosen make this seika informal.

Right Japanese iris, which flower in May, are traditionally used in the Boy's Day (5 May) arrangement. Here Dutch iris have been used instead.

■ ARRANGEMENTS FOR FESTIVALS AND TO MARK THE SEASONS
■ BOYS' DAY ARRANGEMENT

Container: turquoise ceramic container
Material: purple iris with leaves
Method of support: kenzan, hidden by black pebbles

Tango-no-sekku, Boys' or Children's Day, 5 May, is a national holiday in Japan. Families with sons proudly fly *koi-no-bori,* colourful carp-shaped banners on lofty bamboo poles outside their houses and display miniature sets of samurai armour in the tokonoma. *Shōbu* (Japanese iris) are the traditional flower used in a Boys' Day arrangement, expressing the aspiration that sons will grow up straight and strong and brave like the swordlike leaves of the shōbu plant.

■ AN ARRANGEMENT FOR GIRLS' DAY

Container: turquoise compote
Material: pale pink tulips, mimosa (*Acacia dealbata*), pink spray chrysanthemums
Method of support: kenzan

Hinamatsuri, the Doll Festival, is held on Girls' Day, 3 March. Traditional Japanese dolls, of which every self-respecting small Japanese girl has a collection, are displayed on stepped shelves in the tokonoma. The little girls, dressed in *kimono* and themselves looking like little dolls, are taken by their proud parents to visit the local shrine or temple. Girls' Day arrangements should be delicate and feminine and use spring material. Pink and yellow are the customary colours. Pink (traditionally peach) blossoms and yellow daffodils make a pretty combination or, as here, pink tulips and yellow mimosa.

Left Pink and yellow are the colours traditionally associated with Girl's Day. Here pink tulips and chrysanthemums are used with sunny mimosa.

■ SPRING ARRANGEMENTS
■ BOAT AT ANCHOR

Container: boat vase made from the lower part of a bamboo stem, resting on a pair of 'anchors'
Material: *Typha angustifolia* (bulrush), grasses, purple iris, small white 'Micro' spray chrysanthemums
Method of fixing: kenzan

Boat arrangements have long been popular. Containers are made from bronze, bamboo, wood and ceramic. This container, with its curious topknot at the stern end, is a particularly handsome bamboo boat. There are many styles: outgoing boat, homecoming boat and this version, in which the boat rests quietly, its sails furled.

Right The spring winds can be felt in the furled sails of this boat quietly resting at anchor.

Left The dynamic sweeping lines give a sense of powerful movement and potential growth to this spring arrangement.

■ **IN-YO-IKE** (Sun and Shade arrangement)

Container: square, black ceramic container
Material: Azalea branches, pink Kaffir lilies (*Schizostylis coccineus*), conifer
Method of support: kenzan

The small pink Kaffir lilies seem to be growing out of a soft mound of conifer at the heart of this arrangement. The main azalea branch swoops down from the left in a dramatic curve that is extended on the right by the second branch.

■ AUTUMN ARRANGEMENTS
■ SEVEN AUTUMN GRASSES

Container: lacquered bamboo basket

Material: *Miscanthus sinensis* 'Zebrinus' (zebra grass), solidaster, white, mauve and purple Michaelmas daisies (*Aster novii-belgii*) and other grasses

Method of support: kenzan. 'Shoes' cut from thick stem are used to hold and fix thin stems.

The traditional materials for this pretty autumn arrangement are *susuki* grass (*Miscanthus sinensis*), *hagi* (*Lespedeza bicolour* or bush clover), *nadesiko* (*Dianthus superba*), *ominaesi* (*Patrinia scabioso* like Aster *novii-belgii* or Michaelmas daisies), *kikyo* bellflower or *Platycodon grandiflorum, kuzu (Pueraria thunbergia)* and *fuzibakama (Eupatorium)*. The choice of material epitomizes the Japanese taste for the simple and natural, for flowers that are often unappreciated or regarded as weeds, yet most of us respond to the modest, unassuming charm of field flowers and grasses. The material for such an arrangement can easily be gathered on a country walk.

Right This natural arrangement of autumn grasses has a simple charm.

Left Chrysanthemums are highly prized in Japan not only for their flowers but for their leaves. In this seika the beauty of both is seen to advantage.

■ CHRYSANTHEMUMS IN A CHINESE-STYLE BASKET

Container: large-handled black bamboo 'peony' basket
Material: Pale orange single bloom chrysanthemums
Method of fixing: Y-shaped kubari

This traditional seika arrangement gains a much larger presence from being made in this striking basket with its graceful, arching handle. The black bamboo of the basket sets off the pale orange chrysanthemums and the rich green leaves.

Right Bamboo and
pine, symbolizing
resilience and endurance,
are traditional materials
used at New Year.

■ ARRANGEMENT FOR THE NEW YEAR

Container: rectangular, black ceramic moribana container
Material: three pieces of black bamboo, pine, *Skimmia japonica*, *Lilium longiflorum*, pink single-flowered spray chrysanthemums
Method of support: kenzan

New Year is the most important festival in the Japanese calendar. Before the end of the year all outstanding debts are settled, the house is cleaned thoroughly and special food is prepared, enough to last for several days so people will be free to enjoy themselves.

Bamboo and pine are traditional materials used in New Year arrangements; bamboo, because it bends in a gale but does not break, and pine for its ability to survive under the most severe conditions. The hope is that these qualities will be shared by members of the household in the year ahead. Plum, which courageously blossoms even while snow is on the ground, is the third of these 'three friends of winter'. As plum blossom was unavailable little starry, mauve-centred chrysanthemums were used instead. The scarlet berries on the skimmia are another seasonal touch, while the lilies symbolize purity.

◼ CHABANA AND MINIATURE ARRANGEMENTS

Small, inconspicuous, unscented flowers are used in chabana (tea flowers). Sometimes the arrangement comprises only one flower. This is known as an *ichi-rin-ike*. At other times a branch may be used as well.

◼ CHABANA IN A BRONZE VASE

Container: small, bronze Chinese-style vase
Material: *Eupatorium cannabinum* (hemp agrimony)
Method of fixing: bending

This is the ultimate in understatement; tiny, inconspicuous flowers, un-remarkable leaves and yet, set here in this vase for our contemplation, they stir us more deeply than showier flowers. Perhaps we come away more ready to see beauty in unexpected places, in the weed growing between the cracks in broken paving, in light reflected in water caught in a hollow, in shadows playing on a wall. Perhaps too we will be more attentive to the quiet, unassuming people we meet and learn to value qualities not measured in materialistic terms.

Below The symmetry of the vase provides a sharp contrast to the foliage, yet the whole composition is perfectly balanced.

■ CHABANA IN A BASKET

Container: closely woven black bamboo basket
Material: *Forsythia suspensa* and rust-red single-flowered spray chrysanthemums
Method of fixing: bend and balance

A few of the forsythia leaves are just beginning to colour and their hue is picked up and intensified in the petals of the small, yellow-centred chrysanthemums used in this simple chabana.

Below The texture and colour of the bamboo basket provide a good contrast to the foliage and flowers.

▓ A SELECTION OF MINIATURE IKEBANA

Small pots, bottles or jugs are easy to come by and fun to use for miniature arrangements that can be made in a moment, often using flowers and foliage left over from larger arrangements.

Below, from left to right azalea with yellow roses in a bronze bottle; *Spiraea x arguta* and a pink chrysanthemum in an African snuff carrier; sprays of *Spiraea x arguta* with a rust chrysanthemum in a long-necked bottle; broom and 'Blushing Bride' in a Greek jug; mauve freesia in a ceramic pebble pot; tall cotoneaster with a spider chrysanthemum in a ceramic bottle.

■ FREE-STYLE

This is a selection of arrangements to give you ideas. Many of them use exotic material or the familiar in a surprising and innovative way. Others use unusual containers or adapt objects designed for another purpose. Their purpose is to suggest fresh approaches and stimulate your imagination.

■ STRONG VERTICAL MOVEMENT

LINE AND MASS

Container: long ceramic trough with mottled creamy glaze
Material: giant allium flowers; leaves of *Hosta sicboldiana* 'Elegans'
Method of support:· two kenzans

The impact of this arrangement derives largely from the striking material: huge, round allium heads with their soft mass of densely packed multiple blossoms on long straight stalks, elegantly curving, and heart-shaped hosta leaves whose quiet blue-green sets off the textured mauve of the flowers. The design is very simple. Two tall stems reach up from a single point, making a narrow V terminated by the head of the shorter stem. The two flower heads are like two high notes. On the right two flowers cut short – the low notes – stand one behind the other, giving a sense of depth. Crossing from right to left and intersecting the V, the fifth flower dynamically alters the mood, changing it perhaps from classical to jazz. The arching leaves at the base of the stems anchor and link the two groups like a syncopated bass section.

LINE AND FORM

Container: ceramic slab pot randomly glazed in soft blue and brown. Made by author
Material: *Nelumbo nucifera* (lotus) buds and *Gaultheria shallon*
Method of support: pieces of stem inserted crosswise in the container

The form of these buds and the light gleaming on them were so beautiful that all that was required was simply to let them stand quietly in their upward ascent. This was not so easily achieved given the weight of the heads, the length of the stems and the difficulty of working in the extremely narrow vase. It was managed by fixing short lengths of stem, cut to fit across the container and support them. The gaultheria stems were placed to show the leaves in profile so as not to detract from the shape of the buds.

Right Massy mauve alium heads contrast with the vertical and diagonal lines formed by their stems in this arrangement in a low trough.

| **Left** The narrowness of the vase can be seen in the side view. | **Above** Sculptural lotus buds on sinuous stems rise from a vase whose colours suggest the muddy water of a lotus pool. |

LINE AND FORM

Container: metal form of iron rings, bent and sprayed blue. Made by the arranger

Material: silverleaf stems, *Aster novii-belgii* (miniature white Michaelmas daisy), dried and silvered wistaria vine

Method of support: kenzan and support given by container

The most striking feature of this arrangement is the looping calligraphic line made by the wisteria vine. This both extends and contains the two small groups of leaves and flowers, as well as introducing flowing movement into the piece.

The silverleaf tree, whose natural habitat is Table Mountain, near the southern tip of Africa, is named for the silvery appearance of its leaves. This is due to the covering of fine hairs that protects the leaves from excessive transpiration during the hot, dry summer months.

Here the heart of leaves around the bud (which tends to droop) has been plucked out to reveal the starlike ring beneath. Miniature white Michaelmas daisies radiate from the larger stem. A smaller second stem of silverleaf, supported on a kenzan a little to the right, is held within the lower loop of wistaria vine, which has been painted silver.

Right Looping wistaria vine and starry silverleaf are supported by a small blue metal form.

■ A STUDY IN COLOUR, LINE AND SHAPE

Container: abstract container of cut and bent iron, sprayed dark green. Made by arranger

Material: *Castanea sativa* (Spanish chestnut, or marron) stem with fruit, lime green spider chrysanthemum blooms

Method of support: support given by container

The emphatic form and strong colour of the container stabilize the single stem that soars up to end, somewhat apologetically, in a lone and rather disappointingly small fruit. The spidery form and the acid green colour of the magnificent 'Cremona' chrysanthemum at its base acknowledge the shape and colour of the container, a comment repeated in the second bloom lying like a shadow below. The spiky shapes and more subdued green of the cluster of chestnuts on the left are a quieter variation on this theme. With a little imagination this arrangement could be read as an ironic comment on the absurdity of overweening aspiration.

■ DYNAMIC LINE AND ILLUSION

Container: glass perfume bottle
Material: *Acacia erioloba* and white freesia
Method of support: supported by neck of bottle

The combination of the container, a form within a form, with the weird abstract lines made by the thorn branches gives this small arrangement an elegant, somewhat sinister power. What you notice first is the glowing green and golden core of the bottle and the sweeping lines of the reddish acacia stems with their cruel thorns. Only as you continue to look does the actual shape of the vase, held and echoed by the downward curving stems, emerge. And last of all you see the frail unemphatic flower held, as it were, captive in the heart of the arrangement.

Right A frail flower lies captive at the heart of this arrangement.

■ FRUIT SALAD?

Container: shallow glass dish
Material: *Magnolia grandiflora* leaves, *Bryonia dioica* (White Bryony), chrysanthemum petals
Method of support: none used

"It looks like fruit salad!" one young person exclaimed on seeing this picture and, since the point of this style is to use familiar material in an unfamiliar way, it was an appropriate comment.

The inspiration for this arrangement came from the lovely rust-coloured bloom on the underside of the magnolia leaves, which is such a surprising contrast to the glossy green surface. The hollow in the centre of the pale green dish was filled with water and on this pale orange chrysanthemum petals were randomly scattered. Around them the magnolia leaves, cut in half along the spine, were arranged in an unfolding whorl, the velvety undersurface face up. Completing the composition a necklace of scarlet and green bryony berries introduces contrasting shape and texture and an intensity of colour without which this would lack impact and merely be a curiosity.

The arrangement obviously needs to be placed on a low surface so that the design can be appreciated.

Above This arrangement shows how familiar material can be used in an unexpected manner: magnolia leaves have been cut in half and chrysanthemums shredded.

■ SPACE AS PART OF THE DESIGN

Container: three flattened and hollowed-out granite pebbles
Material: *Miscanthus sinensis* 'Zebrinus' (zebra grass), Eucalyptus (red gum) flowers
Method of fixing: supported by container and balanced

This is a striking and elegant design contrasting the rounded shapes of the pebble containers with their subtle tones and the dramatic lines and marking of the zebra grass. Stems of this have been laid horizontally to link the two groups. The small, pink, feathery-soft flowers add colour and variety of shape. We see clearly how space is an integral part of the design.

■ CONTRASTING TEXTURES

Container: wooden bowl made from a large hollowed-out 'oak apple'
Material: *Poncirus trifoliata* (Japanese bitter orange), pine, anthurium

This rich arrangement exploits the wonderfully sensuous texture of the wooden bowl – it is like a giant walnut shell – by contrasting it with the spiky green thorns of the wild orange resting on a dark bed of prickly pine needles. The moulded texture and form of the waxy pink and white anthurium flowers have the same voluptuous quality as the surface of the bowl, while their stamens echo the colour and suggest the form of the thorns on the green branches.

Opposite Horizontally laid grasses unite three small arrangements into one larger composition, incorporating the space between them.

Right The form of the large satiny wooden bowl is complemented by the waxy anthurium flowers while the spiky acid-green thorns add an astringent note.

■ HORIZONTAL AND VERTICAL LINES

Container: pair of interlocking iron forms (made by the arranger) supporting a hexagonal plastic vase

Material: *Pyracantha, Miscanthus sinensis* (susuki grass), stripped and bleached *Buxus sempervirens* (box), pale yellow single-flowered chrysanthemum blooms

Method of support: kenzan and support given by container

The dramatic form of the iron framework with its strong horizontal and vertical lines supports a small hexagonal vase that holds the flowers. With their bold white shape and bright yellow centres, the blossoms are strong enough to hold their own against the powerful base. So too is the spiky mass of pyracantha, which forms the background and assertively reaches forward to the left. Toward the back on the right a creamy white mass of bleached box makes a foil and from it plumes of susuki grass reach forward and up, echoing the colour of the box and softening the arrangement.

Right The dramatic horizontal and vertical lines of the iron support provide a strong visual foundation for this large arrangement.

Left Another large arrangement; its expansive lines suggest autumnal dissolution and its subdued colours convey a sense of disillusion.

■ AUTUMN MOOD

Container: old iron pipe

Material: *Euonymus alata* branches, smoke bush (*Cotinus coggyria*), yellow *Euphorbia fulgens*, red lily, stripped and bleached ivy stems

Method of fixing: supported by container and balanced

The autumnal mood of this arrangement is established by the red-dish euonymus foliage springing out like flames from the smouldering smoke bush at its heart. The half-seen red lily and outreaching pale gold euphorbia stems develop the bonfire image and the ivy wood reaches up to feed the fire.

Right The placement of foliage inside the clear glass of the vase integrates it into the composition. The fluid mass of asparagus fern leads the eye down the arrangement.

■ UNDERWATER

Container: heavy modern glass vase with blue and yellow decorations
Material: *Lilium longiflorum, Asparagus densiflorus* 'Meyen' fern
Method of fixing: none needed

Asparagus fern makes a dense mass at the summit of the arrangement, repeating the form of the vase below. The strong white trumpets of the lilies emerge from this thick greenery with startling effect. Pendulous fronds of looser foliage hang down and link the two centres of the arrangement and smaller pieces of fern are submerged in the water, taking the green down to the very bottom of the vase.

■ IN AND YO BALANCE OF OPPOSITES

Container: two small hexagonal plastic vases
Dried and bleached material: driftwood (pine), *Morus* (mulberry) and *Buxus sempervirens* (box)
Fresh material: *Anigozanthos* (kangaroo paw), *Strelitzia reginae* (bird-of-paradise flower), bear grass
Method of support: kenzan

This composition combines delicacy and strength. The two containers are linked by the dramatic mass of bleached driftwood and by the branch of bleached box that sweeps to the left. Against this background elegant stems of kangaroo paw hold up their small, luminous flowers. On the right a bird-of-paradise flower aligns its beak with the movement of the box, its flame-coloured petals streaming backward and a second flower points directly forward. The interplay of fine grasses arching across the upper spaces makes this a clear example of the in and yo balance of opposites.

Above This large composition is in fact two small arrangements united by driftwood and dry material. Grasses reach across the upper space.

■ GOING FOR SIZE

Container: early vase by Lucie Rie
Dried and bleached material: bamboo root, *Edgeworthia papyrifera (mitsumata)*, *Morus alba* 'pendula' (weeping mulberry)
Fresh material: *Pieris japonica*, spray chrysanthemums, bear grass
Method of fixing: bend and balance
These two pictures show how a simple massed arrangement of flowers, foliage and grasses in a tall vase can be expanded into a dramatic display by the addition of dried material.

Left An arrangement which captures the mood of early spring with its changeable days of sun, wind and showers.

Opposite A stumpy piece of bleached bamboo root has been placed on the right front of the vase, extending and giving weight to the base of the arrangement. Two pieces of weeping mulberry take the design even farther to the right on a higher plane: the lower piece curving out and back on itself to suggest a cloud, the higher one slanting down like a flash of jagged lightning.

Opposite Bottom Here the drama of the storm is seen in full force with the addition of further pieces of bleached wistaria vine, suggesting swirling gusts of wind, and mitsumata laid horizontally like flashes of sheet lightning.

■ SPRING MOOD

Container: multiple vase comprising small pot and small and larger rings

Material: *Syringa vulgaris* (lilac) branches, purple iris, pale pink tulips, fatsia leaf

Method of fixing: balance and support from container (no kenzan is used in this arrangement)

In this arrangement the ends of the branches are cut to fit against the sides of the containers, and their upper branches intertwine like the supports of a wigwam, a balancing feat requiring no mean skill.

The bare lilac branches speak of winter or the cold winds of March, but down below small flowers are springing up in the sheltered lee of the hollow, opening their petals where the sun has warmed the earth.

■ LANDSCAPE ARRANGEMENT

Container: round, unglazed stoneware dish
Method of fixing: two kenzans
Material: small-needled pine, *Polygonatum odoratum* (Solomon's seal), *Arum maculatum* (Lords and Ladies) berries, *gentiana asclepiadea* (Willow gentian), small-leaved evergreen azalea.

An early Ohara arrangement, the landscape style uses scaled-down material to suggest a view. In this 'realistic' version the predominant feature is the small-needled pine branch leaning forward from the main kenzan at the back of the container and extending well beyond its edge. Sheltering at its foot are green and red wild arum berries, a single taller gentian and low sprays of small-leaved azalea. The second kenzan, front-right, supports two elegant stems of Solomon's seal, whose leaves half-conceal and half-reveal further berries and gentians. The overall effect is totally natural, suggesting plants growing beside a woodland pool. The reddening berries and signs of age on the Solomon's seal leaves hint at the approach of autumn and cooler days. The subdued colours are typical of this style.

| **Below left** Landscape arrangement, typical of the Ohara school, suggesting a woodland scene.

| **Right** The side view shows the placement of the two kenzans and the material.

Left Driftwood is invaluable if it is hard to get fresh foliage. Here just a few simple flowers and leaves bring a much-used specimen to life.

Above Side view showing the wood near the front of the container. The material seems to be growing from the kenzan tucked underneath the driftwood.

■ ARRANGEMENT WITH DRIFTWOOD

Container: large round stoneware dish
Method of fixing: two kenzans
Material: driftwood, *Calendula officinalis* (pot marigold), variegated evergreen euonymus

A simple yet striking arrangement, this uses a minimum of material. Notice the fading flower, half-hidden by the wood, kept as a reminder of passing time, while the unopened bud promises another flower.

Right Example of the charming dancing floor style, created to mark the 90th anniversary of the Ohara school in 1985.

■ HANA-MAI (DANCING FLOWERS)

Container: matching pair of turquoise ceramic compotes
Method of fixing: two kenzans
Material: *Weigela florida* 'variegata' kniphofia (red hot pokers)
A very different style, this Dancing Flower arrangement was created in 1985 to mark the Ohara School's 90th anniversary by Natsuki Ohara, headmaster-designate. The material is supported on two kenzan placed asymmetrically opposite near the edge of the container or, as here, in two separate containers. Long stems reach up, leaning toward one another to touch or cross off-centre near their tips. This dymamic, joyful style is full of movement and energy.

Left The weight of clear dramatic line is balanced by the mass of gerbera.

■ LINE AND MASS

Container: abstract free-style compote with three apertures
Material: white gerbera and while allium (onion flowers)
Method of fixing: kenzan

This lively composition exploits the dynamic lines of the mop-headed allium flowers. The low position of the two gerbera anchors the arrangement, giving it stability as well as enhancing its visual impact. The graphic lines of this work, contrasted with the dense masses of the flowers, make this an arrangement of great interest and energy.

Note: The allium stems were tied together while growing to produce this unusual effect.

■ FIRST BUNJIN-IKE ARRANGEMENT

Container: lion-handled, Chinese-style vase on black-lacquer shiki-ita
Material: mauve hydrangeas, *Colutea arborescens* (Bladder Senna), montbretia leaves
Method of fixing: bending

The main line reaches forward and left as far as the edge of the base the vase rests on. The colutea leaves contrast with its seed pods and are highlighted by a few flowers. Three montbretia leaves support this line. The soft mauve of the hydrangea heads forms a mass of summer colour and gives weight.

▌**Above** The side view not only shows how far forward the main lines reach but reveals the surprising backward movement of one branch of colutea.

▌**Right** This is an example of a bunjin-ike or literati style arrangement, a 19th-century which has been revived by the Ohara school.

■ SECOND BUNJIN-IKE ARRANGEMENT

Container: square nageire vase, copy of a classical Chinese shape used with a black-lacquer shiki-ita

Material: *Acer palmatum* (Japanese maple), 'stargazer' lily, small-needled pine

Method of fixing: bending

This sparkling arrangement so places the starry leaves of Japanese maple that they are seen to maximum effect, each clear-cut shape a variation on its neighbours. The lily, following the left and forward movement of the main line, repeats the star motif in a more emphatic form, while sharp, bright pine needles add further brilliance. The lines on the container suggest light flaking off gently rocking water and the dark pool of the lustrous lacquer shiki-ita suggests the quieter still water beyond the reflected light.

Treatment of maple: Wrap branches to protect the leaves, dip the ends briefly in boiling water, then steep in cold water. They like a little gin or vodka added to the water.

Above left Another very pleasing example of a bunjin-ike.

Above In the side view all the material is seen to lean forward.

Above The side view reveals the full dramatic sweep of the clematis.

Right Flowers placed so that they seem to be growing naturally; this is the aim in nageire and here it has been perfectly achieved.

■ FLOWING NAGEIRE STYLE

Container: free-form nageire vase with streaky turquoise glaze
Material: purple clematis Ernest Markham and *Foeniculum vulgare* (fennel)
Method of support: clematis fixed into split chopstick used as drop-stick
Treatment of clematis: cut and singe stems until blackened, then stand in water for two to three hours or overnight. Recut stems before using. In this elegant composition, the graceful leaves of the clematis vine seem to be floating on a gentle breeze. The flowers, in different stages of development, are placed to show their chalicelike profile and handsome crown of stamens ringing the heart. The pale yellow umbel of feathery-leaved fennel adds height and balances the downward curve of the clematis.

■ VIEWING MOUNT FUJI

Container: small black lacquer bucket decorated with leaping carp
Material: purple Dutch iris and *Salix matsudana* 'Tortuosa' (contorted willow)
Method of support: kenzan

This comprises a simple spring arrangement. The rustic bucket shape expressed in sophisticated lacquerwork gives the container a piquancy. On the left two iris reach up, the taller bud leaning slightly to the right. Extending much farther right the delicate contorted willow peaks and falls away, suggesting distantly viewed Mount Fuji, the most famous view in Japan.

Above The willow branch in this simple spring arrangement was chosen because its shape suggested the peak of Mount Fuji.

Above Here the two containers are slightly separated to suggest the opening of the screen's panels. Arching montbretia leaves bridge the gap so that they still form a single arrangement. Yet by this simple action a fresh, more open composition has been created.	**Top** This is a Rimpa arrangement, a long low style created by the headmaster of the Ohara school, which was inspired by the screen paintings of Ogata Körin.

■ AN ARRANGEMENT INSPIRED BY A PAINTED SCREEN

Container: matching pair of curved Shigaraki containers on low feet
Material: pink hydrangea and astilbe, montbretia leaves, hosta, *Spirea x arguta*
Method of fixing: five kenzans

Rimpa is a long, low 'running' style created by Houn Ohara, headmaster of the Ohara School, and inspired by the screen paintings of Ogata Kōrin. In this example five types of material are used. The low curving line of the containers is punctuated by irregular masses of pink hydrangeas, the painter's brush — as it were — fully loaded with paint and brought down in soft, full strokes. The softer feathery-pink exclamations of astilbe are drawn with a more careful brush, the light touches of spirea with yet more delicate strokes. Then, very delicately indeed and with the barest touch of paint, the curving lines of montbretia are traced in. Finally, the brush is dipped again, where the colour has concentrated, and the stronger tones of hosta are added for emphasis.

■ A LINEAR ARRANGEMENT

Container: white ceramic trough with two horizontal black lines
Material: *Lavatera trimestus*, white gerbera, pampas grass
Method of fixing: two kenzans

Here the characteristic three-dimensional aspect of ikebana is restricted, making it a practical style for a position with limited depth or where people pass by close in front.

In this summery arrangement the upward movement of the lavatera, used for the main line on the left, is echoed and relaxed in the only slightly shorter right-hand line. Two white gerbera form the third line. Pampas grasses form an arching tracery linking the two groups.

Above From the side the restricted depth of this arrangement is evident.

Left Summery linear-style arrangement in a trough; a style which suits a narrow space since the material does not reach far forward.

■ HARMONIZING COLOURS

Container: rectangular, black moribana container
Material: *Ribes odorata* (Buffalo currant) branches, red lily
Method of fixing: kenzan

The lower branches of *Ribes odorata* sweeps forward from the left, low across the water. A few leaves are already turning scarlet. Behind it the second branch diverges, holding a single leaf aloft. On the left a deep red-orange lily leans forward, with a bud reaching out to the left.

| **Above** Here orange lilies harmonize with autumn tints in the foliage used. | **Above right** Vivid orange lilies contrast with the strong purple container in this small free-style arrangement. |

■ CONTRASTING COLOURS

Container: Semicircular plastic container designed by Soegtsu head-master, Sofu Teshigahara
Material: wisteria and red 'Harvest' lily
Method of fixing: kenzan

The inspiration for this arrangement came from the strong purple colour of the container. Deep orange 'Harvest' lilies were chosen to challenge and wisteria to palely echo its deep purple. The elegant mauve wisteria panicles arch above the drooping leaves. The lilies, contrasting strongly in colour and shape, are placed showing the uppermost flower in profile.

■ MASKING DOMINANT MATERIAL

Container: rustic unglazed ceramic vase
Material: *Chaenomeles japonica* (Japanese quince) with fruit, 'Stargazer' lily.
Method of fixing: bend and balance

The green fruits on the branch that reaches forward on the right are just flushed with pink. This colour is intensified by the lily, half-hidden behind the leftward-leaning side branch. Fully seen the flower would be too dominant. The container – with its rough, pinky-brown surface – is well chosen to go with this material.

■ USING CAST-OFF FLOWERS

Container: buff-coloured ceramic vase, with contrasting interior, on three low feet
Material: three hosta leaves, 'Stargazer' lily with bud
Method of fixing: kenzan

This arrangement shows what can be made out of virtually nothing if we learn to recognize its potentiality. The colour and texture of the leaves, the shape of the unopened bud, the colours of the open flower and the wide expanse of water all suggest the lotus, material, hence making indirect reference to the plant so closely associated with Buddha. A story tells how Buddha, being asked to explain the meaning of life and how to transcend its unavoidable pain and suffering, answered by picking a lotus blossom and wordlessly holding it up to his disciples. The lotus plant grows in the muddiest ponds, rooting in the dirt and detritus that collect at the bottom. From this its stems grow up through the murky water, bearing buds that open into flowers of breathtaking purity and unsullied beauty.

Below left A large lily which would otherwise dominate this small arrangement is masked, leaving the attention free to dwell on the branch and its fruit where the pink of the lily is subtly echoed.

Below When you trim material, do not throw away rejected flowers and leaves. This modest but graceful arrangement was created from just such cast-offs.

FINDING AND CHOOSING MATERIAL

The question of what material to use and where to find it needs some thought. If you are lucky enough to have a garden, you will always be able to find something in it to use. Suggestions for plants to grow are given below.

For many people flowers are less of a problem than branches, so we will start with the easier of the two. If you must rely on bought material, then the first thing to do is to find and estabish a good relationship with a sympathetic florist. Unless you can buy them when they are still fresh, flowers will not keep so well.

Tell the florist about your interest and the kind of material you are looking for and get his or her advice. Material used in the arrangements in this book will give some idea what to ask for. Most florists do not stock a wide range of branches, but a good florist should welcome your interest and be willing to order material for you. It is also worth finding out what days they get fresh stock in.

As far as possible buy flowers in bud and with long stems. Check the leaves and reject flowers in which there are signs of wilting or yellowing. If leaves have been removed from chrysanthemums or lilies it probably means they have been around for a while. When you have decided on your purchase, make sure that the flower heads are well protected when wrapped so that you can get them home without any damage. As soon as you are home, strip off the lower leaves, cut the ends under water and stand them in water in a bucket or tall vase in a cool place to recover for at least an hour before arranging. In hot weather – or if they are at all tired-looking – spray with water from a mister.

Initially single flowers are easier to work with. In springtime tulips, iris, daffodils, anemones and narcissus are widely available. Many flowers, including tulips and iris, like a little sugar in the water.

If tulips droop, wrap the whole length, including the heads, in newspaper and stand in water to which a little detergent has been added.

If you have bought irises in bud and do not want to use them immediately, stand in water without cutting. They will start to open as soon as they are cut.

Limp-necked anemones should revive if wrapped to cover the heads and stood in hot water up to their necks for about 10 minutes. Then plunge into cold water. This also encourages flowers to open.

Chrysanthemums, lilies and carnations are generally available throughout the year and usually last well, provided they have not been in the shop for too long. Remove the lower leaves and cut and crush the stems before putting in water.

Roses are unpredictable. Remove the thorns and lower leaves, cut under water and stand in deep water for at least an hour. If the heads droop wrap them, and cut and then plunge the stems into boiling water with a little sugar added for five minutes. Put straight into deep cold water and leave overnight if possible. This method can also be used with hydrangeas, dahlias, chrysanthemums and other daisylike flowers.

The stems of certain flowers – like Iceland poppies, clematis, euphorbia and other plants that exude a milk – should be singed in a flame, taking care to protect the heads, then plunged into deep cold water.

If you are picking your own material, do so when the weather is cool. The best time is early morning before the sun is on the plants. Cut stems long and have a bucket of water nearby so that you can put the flowers and branches straight in. Splitting the ends of branches makes it easier for them to absorb water.

SUGGESTIONS FOR PLANTS

Obviously this list cannot be comprehensive. The plants suggested have been chosen because they are easy to grow, last well in an arrangement and will enhance your garden. Most shrubs and trees, and flowers too, are encouraged to grow by being cut, but they must be reasonably well-established first.

FOR BASIC GENERAL ARRANGEMENTS

Aucuba Japonica (spotted laurel), a vigorous grower, has big strong leaves and is useful in a large arrangement.

Azalea flowers are lighter and more elegant, as is their foliage, which deepens to wine or golden hues in autumn. Like rhododendron, the flowers come in many colours.

Broom *(Sarothamnus scoparius)* bends easily into elegant lines. It is a useful material all year round with the bonus of colour when it is in flower. Along with the common yellow wild variety, broom is available in a lovely range of pinks, lemons, golds and rusts, as well as white. This, incidentally, is the *planta genista* that the Plantagenets took their name from, and it is also the flower of Brittany. It also is good for free-style arrangements.

Camellia is slow-growing but a good investment both for its foliage, handsome all year, and its glorious pink, white or red flowers.

Chaenomeles japonica (Japanese quince) is slow-growing but is well worth the wait with its angular branches, pale pink or brick-red flowers, and fruits that, from green, flush pink and then gold in autumn. It is lovely against a white-washed wall.

Cotoneaster 'Cornubia' has small white flowers in spring but its time of glory is autumn, when its sturdy branches are thick with bright orange berries.

Fatsia japonica, an equally strong plant, has bright green palmate leaves ideal for free-style work.

Forsythia is spectacular in spring, with its bright yellow flowers on bare branches, and lovely again in autumn when the leaves mellow to soft pinks and golds.

Gaultheria is a hardy shrub supplying handsome, long-lasting foliage for most of the year.

Hosta, of which there are many varieties, has heart-shaped leaves valued for masking the kenzan and also for their elegant shape.

Ligustrum (privet) is a great standby from spring through to autumn. The variegated varieties *(ovalifolium Aureum and 'Aureovariegatum')* are much prettier than the common dark green *vulgare*.

Mahonia japonica or aquifolium (Oregon grape), with its elegant pinnate leaves, is also useful for larger displays.

Mespilus germanica (medlar) has strong branches and foliage for larger work, pink or white flowers in spring and curious brown fruit in autumn.

Pine is essential for New Year and small pieces add a sparkle to spring arrangements. Choose a variety with smaller erect needles and strong branches. *Pinus sylvestris* (the Scots pine), or *Pinus mugo* (the mountain pine) are good varieties. Prune to prevent it from growing too large.

Prunus sp. You should have at least one blossom tree — cherry, plum, peach or pear — for spring arrangements. If you decide on a cherry, which will give you pretty fruits to use later on, choose one with single flowers and for preference a delicate colour, such as *Prunus avis*, the bird cherry. The autumn foliage of many of these is also attractive.

Pussy Willow can be easily grown from cuttings — you may even find a stem starting to root in an arrangement — and is lovely spring material. It is easy to shape for windswept styles and freestyle work. There are many kinds, those with reddish or greenish stems being particularly attractive.

Rhododendron provides strong foliage all year and spectacular flowers in early summer. Some have dramatically variegated leaves.

Ribes sanguineum (flowering currant) has dainty leaves and pretty, astringent-scented flowers in the spring. The foliage of **Ribes odorata** (Buffalo currant) is lovely in autumn.

Viburnum tinus is good for masking the kenzan and can also be used for main branches. It has small dark leaves and clusters of pink buds opening into tiny white flowers. Unfortunately it often has a rank unpleasant smell so it may need a thorough washing before use.

■ DRY MATERIAL AND WOOD

Dry material is mainly used in free-style work. Some material you can dry yourself. Dock, teasels, poppy-heads, sea holly, hogweed and its relatives, Chinese lanterns *(Physalis franchettii)* and many grasses dry easily if tied loosely in bunches and hung up in a dry, airy space. Use unperfumed hairspray to defer disintegration.

Beaches and estuaries may be scoured for driftwood. Go after high tide, especially a spring tide, or after a storm. The salt water acts as a preservative so this wood should need no treatment.

Old wood picked up in forests is likely to be damp, rotten and insect-infested, but roots have interesting shapes and a better chance of being in good condition. When cleaned they often prove worth the effort.

Willow branches can be stripped quite easily. Loosen the bark with a sharp knife and, if green, the bark will come away with a good tug. The naked branches can be very effective.

Many department stores and most florists sell dry material, and there are even shops which sell only this.

■ GLOSSARY

A

Adachi modern school of ikebana
aiki-dō Japanese martial art

B

bunjin-bana literati flowers; a style popular in the 19th century
bunjin-ike literati-style arrangement

C

chabana flowers arranged for the tea ceremony
cha-dō the Way of Tea; the tea ceremony
chi the earth; also, breath or spirit

D

dō way or path of personal development
dobōshu arbiters of taste, a profession that arose in the 16th century whose members selected beautiful objects, designed gardens and so on for wealthy clients

E

Enshū classical ikebana school founded in 17th century

F

fusuma internal sliding doors used to divide rooms in a traditional house
futon bedding, floor mattress
fuzibakama Eupatorium sinensis; one of the seven autumn grasses

G

gaku book-learning; theory
geisha courtesan; highly trained hostess and entertainer
getsu the moon
gyō semiformal

H

hagi Lespedeza bicolour, or bush clover; one of the seven autumn grasses
hana branches and flowers, material used in ikebana
hana-mai dancing flowers, an Ohara School style
hara the solar plexus
hasami ikebana scissors
hinamatsuri Doll Festival held on Girls' Day, 3 March

I

ichi-mon-ji-dome single-bar fixing used in nageire arrangements
ichi-rin-ike single-flower arrangement
Ichiyo a modern school of ikebana
iemoto headmaster of ikebana or other, eg tea ceremony, school
ike flower arrangement
ikebana the art of flower arrangement
ike-no-bō hut near the pond; also see next entry
Ikenobō the earliest school of ikebana
ikiru to live; living
in yin; opposite and complementary of yō; female, soft, passive
isshu-ike arrangement using only one type of material

J

jin man, humankind
ju-dō Japanese martial art
jugoya 15th day of the month; autumn moon-viewing festival
jū-ji (cross) crossed-bar fixing for nageire arrangements
jutsu technique; skills

K

ka flowers and branches
kadai a wooden or bamboo base used under a vase
ka-dō the way of flowers; ikebana
kadomatsu New Year decoration of pine, bamboo, folded paper etc, placed at the entrance of the house
kakejiku scroll with calligraphy hung in the tokonama
kami nature spirits; nature gods
karate-dō Japanese martial art
ken sword
ken-dō the way of the sword; Japanese martial art
kenzan pinholder for supporting flowers and branches
kenzan-naoshi tool for cleaning and repairing kenzan
kikyo Platycodon grandiflorum or bellflower; one of the seven autumn grasses
kimono traditional Japanese garment
koan an enigmatic question; Zen technique used as aid to bring about enlightenment
koi-no-bori carp-shaped flags flown on Boys' Day, 5 May
Koryu classical ikebana school
kubari support for holding material in nageire arrangement
kuzu Pueraria thunbergia (Kudzu vine); one of the seven autumn grasses
kyu-dō the Way of Archery; Japanese martial art

M

maki-ashi a wooden base with scrolled ends used to support a vase

matcha thick powdered green tea for tea ceremony

matsuri a festival

mikan Japanese orange similar to a mandarin orange

minakuchi the Water Gate Festival

mitsugusoku the traditional three offerings made to Buddha: fire, flowers and incense

mitsumata dried, stripped and bleached *Edgeworthia papyrifera* branches used in freestyle arrangements

moribana arrangement made in a shallow container

morimono arrangement with fruit and vegetables

moru to pile up

N

nadesiko *Dianthus superba;* one of the seven autumn grasses

nageire informal arrangement made in a cylinder vase

nageire-bana nageire flowers

nichi the sun

nichi-getsu linked round and crescent-shaped kenzan

niju-ike double-mouthed bamboo vase

nishu-ike classical arrangement in double-mouthed vase

O

Ohara modern ikebana school founded in 1895

ominaesi *Patrinia scabiosaefolia;* one of the seven autumn grasses

R

rikka formal classical style dating from 16th century and symbolically representing a landscape

rimpa Ohara School style inspired by the screen paintings by Ogata Korin

ryū school

S

sake Japanese rice wine

samurai class of warriors, ranking below the nobility and above merchants in feudal Japanese society

seika formal classical style dating from the 18th century

shiki-hana laid flowers arranged directly on a table

shiki-ita flat wooden or bamboo base to go under a vase

shimputai modern Ikenobo style

shin formal; also Koryu School name for Line 1

Shintō the indigenous, nature-worshipping religion of Japan

shippo support of interlocking rings used by Ohara School

shōbu Japanese iris; *Iris laevigata*

shoji paper screen used on windows of traditional houses

shōka Ikebono School name for seika style

shu red-orange colour

so informal

so-egi-dome drop-stick support for nageire style

Sogetsu modern ikebana school founded in 1926

sunabachi sand basin, low rectangular bronze vase

sunanomono rikka style made in a sunamono

sushi little cakes of vinegared rice either topped with slices of raw fish, or wrapped in seaweed around pieces of raw or pickled vegetables; eaten with soya sauce and green mustard

susuki *Miscanthus sinensis;* one of the seven autumn grasses

T

tai Line 2 (Koryu School)

taisaku huge, modern freestyle ikebana arrangement

tango-no-sekku Boys' Day festival, 5 May

tansu wooden chest of drawers

tatami thick mats of tightly packed rice straw with a finely woven rush surface, used as floor covering and a unit of measurement in traditional houses

tatebana standing flower style

ten heaven

tenmoku deep brown glaze with rust-coloured highlights popular for teaware and flower vases

tokonoma display alcove in a traditional Japanese room

tome Line 3 (Koryu School)

tsuribana hanging arrangement

tsuri-tsuki hanging moon-shaped vase

tsurute type of ikebana scissors

U

uki-bana floating flowers

usubata bronze container for rikka style

W

wa inner peace

warabi type of ikebana scissors

Y

yō yang; opposite and complementary to yin; active, strong, male, etc

Z

zazen sitting meditation practised in Zen Buddhism

Zen austere Japanese form of Buddhism